Creative Encounters

CREATIVE ENCOUNTERS

ACTIVITIES TO EXPAND CHILDREN'S RESPONSES TO LITERATURE

Anne T. Polkingharn and Catherine Toohey
Illustrated by Lynn Welker

LIBRARIES UNLIMITED, INC.
Littleton, Colorado
1983

LIBRARIES UNLIMITED, INC.
P. O. Box 263
Littleton, Colorado 80160-0263

Library of Congress Cataloging in Publication Data

Polkingharn, Anne T., 1937-
    Creative encounters.

    Bibliography: p. 127
    Includes index.
    1. Children--Books and reading. 2. Children's
literature--Bibliography. 3. Creative activities and
seat work. 4. Story-telling. I. Toohey, Catherine,
1949-   . II. Title.
Z1037.P79   1983   028.5'5   83-8005
ISBN 0-87287-371-4

*To the people and the environment of Harbor Day
School and the "M and M's" who sustained us.*

Preface

We have written this book to provide teachers, librarians, and reading specialists with creative ideas for extending children's literature beyond the story hour and the curriculum. It is intended for people who work with children in grades K–6. Harlequins dancing around the walls of the classroom, special toothpaste for a king, and chameleons that blend with wallpaper are only three of over 50 diverse ideas that involve the child with good literature beyond the initial reading of the story. The child who makes a "microwave bird" from a feather is learning about structure; the one who draws a whingdingdilly from clues in the text is developing listening skills. All of the ideas encourage the child to think about meaning. The titles we have chosen for this book have become the best remembered and most popular in our library.

"Research evidence shows us that experiences provided through literature add measurably to children's store of knowledge, enrich their use of language, and increase their ability to read."[1]

The activities in this book require ordinary classroom materials which will be used to help children reason, draw, write, research, practice language patterns, and discover personal interpretations of the literature. They do not call for comprehension questions at the end of the chapter or ditto sheets of fill-in-the-blank questions. In short, they are fun.

These exercises are designed to allow children to express their creativity in a way inspired by a particular book. The child's imagination is guided by responses to the author's ideas, not by the restrictions of a busy-work project. The results reflect the uniqueness and inventiveness of the children who created them. We encourage children to develop personal literary tastes—to read books they enjoy and to discover new titles and authors.

Using our experiences as a librarian and a classroom teacher, we have conducted workshops for the past eight years and have met with enthusiastic responses from educators all over the United States. They are eager to hear about individual book titles children enjoy, and to acquire creative, inexpensive ideas they can take directly back to their classrooms or libraries. Out of the more than 200 separate ideas we have developed over the years, we have included here over 50 titles and original ideas we have found successful for using books with children. We consider the following qualities in choosing a book for our program:

> The storytelling ability of the author
>
> Originality
>
> Plot
>
> Characterization
>
> Appropriateness of illustration
>
> Format and total appearance of the book

We share respect for the child's interest. Will the book appeal to the child's intelligence and imagination? Does it help him or her understand himself or herself and others? Does it provide pleasure beyond the mastery of basic reading skills? Can reluctant and gifted readers participate and enjoy the book?

---

[1] Bernice Cullinan and Carolyn Carmichael, eds., *Literature and Young Children* (Urbana, IL: National Council of Teachers of English, 1977), p. vii.

This book is arranged so that each entry includes a summary of the story line of one particular book, introduces a related activity, discusses the materials which will be needed, and provides step-by-step instructions for completing the activity. The Notes section includes additional teacher suggestions and related book titles. Bibliographic information for books mentioned in the Notes section is given in the bibliography at the end of the book.

Our experience with using these activities indicates that success depends on following a few simple procedures. First, we read the book ourselves. If we feel enthusiastic about it, then we introduce it to the children. Craft materials for the activity are assembled. We read the book to the entire group, sharing all the illustrations, and then we explain the procedure steps. These steps should be adapted for different age groups and teaching environments. Children are given time to do the project, allowing for individualized responses. We check to see that the children comprehend the book as well as activity directions. Each child's response will and should be different. After completing the activity, each child shares his/her ideas and work with the group. We display the children's work on a bulletin board with the written title of the book. This reinforces the book/project activity association.

The benefits of "real books" and child involvement are tremendous. Children are introduced to reading in a positive manner and are encouraged through the activities to participate in the story. Reading is not seen as an isolated activity but as related to thinking, writing, and connecting ideas with personal experiences.

Table of Contents

Preface 7

If the Dinosaurs Came Back 11
The Princess and the Pea 13
The King's Flower 15
Harold and the Purple Crayon 17
Please Send a Panda 19
Corduroy and *A Pocket for Corduroy* 21
Flat Stanley 24
The Little Red Balloon 26
The 329th Friend 28
Mr. Tamarin's Trees 30
A House Is a House for Me 32
The Pumpkin Smasher 35
The Bump in the Night 37
There's an Ant in Anthony 41
A Perfect Nose for Ralph 43
The Maggie B. 46
The Bed Just So 48
Santa Makes a Change 49
A Book of Hugs 52
The Christmas Cookie Sprinkle Snitcher 55
Families 57
I'm Terrific 60
The Whingdingdilly 62
A Color of His Own 64
"Elmer: The Story of a Patchwork Elephant" 67
Harlequin and the Gift of Many Colors 70
Eight Ate a Feast of Homonym Riddles 72
One Fine Day 73
Tooth-Gnasher Superflash 76
The Aminal 78
My Very Own Octopus 80
Strega Nona 82
Rapunzel 85
There's a Nightmare in My Closet 87

Owl's New Cards 89

Pezzettino 90

My Daddy's Mustache 92

The Field of Buttercups 95

Annie's Rainbow 97

Dear Hildegarde 99

The Biggest Sandwich Ever 102

Crictor 105

The Lonely Skyscraper 107

Humbug Rabbit 109

Benjamin's 365 Birthdays 112

Look Again 114

Red Riding Hood: Retold in Verse for Boys and Girls to Read Themselves 116

Would You Rather 119

The Seamstress of Salzburg 121

The Ice Cream Cone Coot and Other Rare Birds 123

True or False? 125

Bibliography 127

Index 137

If the Dinosaurs Came Back

Bernard Most

(Harcourt Brace Jovanovich, 1978)

This story imagines what it would be like if the dinosaurs came back and how helpful they could be. They could help firemen with fires and provide ski slopes and beach rides for children. This is a very imaginative picture book for storytelling. Dinosaur lovers will respond to the ideas presented.

PURPOSE:

After looking at the illustrations and reading the story, each child imagines what our world would be like if the dinosaurs returned and thinks of ways in which they could be helpful.

MATERIALS:

(1) 12x18-inch piece of white construction paper
(1) 9x12-inch piece of purple or lavender construction paper
Black marking pen or crayon
Glue
Scissors
Dinosaur shapes (if available)

LET'S BEGIN:

1. Read *If the Dinosaurs Came Back*.
2. Trace or draw a dinosaur shape on the purple paper.

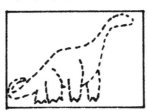

3. Cut and glue the dinosaur shape on the white paper.

4. Think of your own idea of how a dinosaur could be helpful if one came back today.
5. Draw a picture showing how your dinosaur could help in today's world.

6. Print on the picture a caption, "If the dinosaurs came back they _____."

NOTES:

Encourage the children to use different types of dinosaurs. The chart at the end of the book is helpful as the dinosaur shapes are simply outlined.

Display the dinosaur sentences and pictures on a bulletin board or make them into a class book.

Related books:

Dinosaur Funny Bones, by Jean Polhamus (poetry)

Dinosaur's Housewarming Party, by Norma Klein

If I Rode a Dinosaur, by Miriam Young

Quiet on Account of a Dinosaur, by Jane Thayer

Other Books by Bernard Most:

My Very Own Octopus

There's an Ant in Anthony

There's an Ape in the Drape

Dinosaur cookie cutters are available in many kitchen stores and mail-order catalogs.

The Princess and the Pea

Hans Christian Andersen

(Seabury, 1978)

A favorite fairy tale of a prince's search for a "real" princess. During a storm, a girl arrives at the castle claiming to be a princess despite her bedraggled looks. The queen mother devises a clever way to prove the princess' claim. Everyone is delighted with the results and the real princess and prince live in fairy-tale happiness forever after.

PURPOSE:

This activity inspires children to recreate the princess' bed using a split pea.

MATERIALS:

(1) 9x12-inch piece of white construction paper
(1) split pea
Crayons or marking pens
Glue

LET'S BEGIN:

1. Read *The Princess and the Pea*.
2. Glue the split pea on the sheet of paper near the bottom of the page.

3. Design your bed frame (remember 20 mattresses and 20 featherbeds) with high posters.

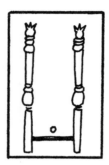

4. Begin adding and designing mattresses and quilts using a different color and pattern for each layer.
5. Draw a "wide awake" princess at the top of your "designer" featherbeds.

NOTES:

Younger children will not be able to count or draw exactly 20 mattresses and 20 featherbeds but will be happy with the bed piled high.

Send children home with a split pea to place under their own mattress.

This project can easily be adapted to a large class mural. To make a mural, use a five-foot piece of butcher paper. Precut 40 smaller strips of paper for the quilts. Let each child decorate a strip. Draw a simple bed frame on the butcher paper. Glue the quilts designed by the children on the bed frame. Be sure to add a princess and the pea.

Related book:
   The Princess on the Nut: Or the Curious Courtship of the Princess on the Pea, by Michelle Nikly

Introduce other fairy tales by Hans Christian Andersen.

The King's Flower

Mitsumasa Anno

(Philomel, 1979)

A king wants the biggest clock, the biggest chocolate bar, the biggest birdcage, etc., for himself. The king soon discovers that biggest is not always better or best. This delightful fable makes fun of pomp and pretense.

PURPOSE:

The king's exaggerated possessions inspire the children to enlarge an ordinary object following the theme of *The King's Flower*.

MATERIALS:

(1) 12x18-inch piece of light colored paper
(1) 2x2-inch piece of gold foil or yellow paper
Crown pattern
Crayons or marking pens
Glue
Scissors

LET'S BEGIN:

1. Read *The King's Flower*. Draw attention to the pictures that depict the king's out-of-scale possessions.
2. Trace the pattern of the king's crown on the foil or yellow paper and cut it out.
3. Glue the crown in the lower left-hand corner of the paper approximately four inches from the bottom of the page.
4. Draw the king's body and robe beneath the crown.

5. Think of a possession this king would love to have.

6. Draw this object, making it very, very large so that it fills most of the rest of the paper. Example: the king's comb, the king's pencil, or the king's calculator.

7. Fill in the details of the king's palace or any other background you feel is appropriate.
8. Share your idea with the group, saying, "This is the king's _____ ."

NOTES:

The fleur-de-lis design is around every page in the book as a decorative border. This design was used by the kings of France and is a symbol of royalty. Some claim it means "flower of Louis," while others claim it means "flower of the lily." Some children may choose to use the fleur-de-lis design as a border or as part of their drawing.

A book introducing the concept of size:
 Let's Find Out What's Big and What's Small, by Martha and Charles Shapp

Other books by Mitsumasa Anno are:
 Anno's Alphabet: An Adventure in Imagination

 Anno's Counting Book

 Anno's Journey

Harold and the Purple Crayon

Crockett Johnson

(Harper & Row, 1955)

Harold is a little boy with a magic purple crayon. He draws his adventures and delightful escapades with his favorite color. His magic crayon draws him safely home at the end of the story.

PURPOSE:

Each child chooses a color and draws an adventure which has been experienced or imagined.

MATERIALS:

(1) 4x18-inch piece of white construction paper
(1) crayon

LET'S BEGIN:

1. Read *Harold and the Purple Crayon*.
2. Discuss the adventures of Harold and establish some creative ideas from the group about other adventures you might include.
3. Choose your favorite color of crayon.
4. Place the paper lengthwise.
5. At the top of the paper, write your name and the color of the crayon you chose. Example: Amy and the Red Crayon.

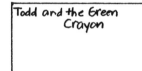

6. Beginning on the left-hand side of the paper, draw your own adventures with your crayon choice.

NOTES:

Younger children will enjoy telling their crayon adventure to the class.

Older children may write a story to go along with their adventure.

Put all the crayon adventures into a class book titled Adventures in Color.

A 16mm film of *Harold and the Purple Crayon* is available from Weston Woods.

Related books about color:

The Chalk Box Story, by Don Freeman

The Great Blueness and Other Predicaments, by Arnold Lobel

How the World Got Its Color, by Marilyn Hirsh

The Night the Crayons Talked, by Vic Knight

Some other titles in the Harold series:

Harold's ABC

Harold's Circus

Harold's Trip to the Sky

A Picture for Harold's Room

This is a good introduction to the primary colors, color wheels and names for unusual colors.

Please Send a Panda

Ruth Orbach

(Philomel, 1977)

A little girl, Agatha, wants an extraordinary pet for her birthday but realizes some animals are not practical. Her grandmother has a solution to her dilemma.

Nov. 26

Dear Grandmother,
   I wish I had a pet pelican. I would feed it fish. It would carry my books in its pouch.
   Love,
   Tracy

PURPOSE:

Children can imagine having a very "extraordinary" pet of their own choosing. The writing and sharing of letters is an individual as well as a group activity.

MATERIALS:

(1) sheet of notebook paper
Black marking pen or pencil

LET'S BEGIN:

1. Read *Please Send a Panda*.
2. Imagine a very EXTRAORDINARY pet that you would like to have.
3. Write a letter to your grandmother asking for this extraordinary pet, telling her why you would like to have it and how you would care for it.

4. Draw the pet you chose on the letter.
5. Share your letter and ideas with the class.

NOTES:

Letter writing form can be practiced. Show the letters that Agatha wrote to her grandmother.

As a follow-up, children can go to the library and do research on the animal they have chosen.

Research questions:

What does the animal eat?

What climate does it need or like?

Describe the habitat of the animal.

Would your animal need a pen, cage, small space, large space, leash, etc.?

Would your animal be happy living with you? Would you encounter some of the problems Agatha had?

What problems might your extraordinary pet cause?

Related books:

The Boy with a Billion Pets, by Peggy Mann

The Fish from Japan, by Elizabeth Cooper

No Place for a Goat, by Helen Sattler

Your Pet Beaver, by Bobbie Hamsa

Your Pet Camel, by Bobbie Hamsa

Your Pet Elephant, by Bobbie Hamsa

Your Pet Kangaroo, by Bobbie Hamsa

Your Pet Penguin, by Bobbie Hamsa

Corduroy

Don Freeman

(Viking, 1968)

This is a story of a stuffed bear living in a department store and waiting for someone to take him home. Corduroy is missing a button on his green overalls and has quite an adventure searching for one. Lisa buys Corduroy and gives him a home, a new button, and friendship.

A Pocket for Corduroy

Don Freeman

(Viking, 1978)

This is a further adventure for Corduroy and Lisa. Corduroy searches for a pocket in the laundromat and ends up spending a very exciting night there. When Lisa finds her friend, she sews a pocket on his overalls and tucks a name card inside.

PURPOSE:

This activity recounts Corduroy's adventures in both books and allows the children to make their own paper bear.

MATERIALS:

(1) 9x12-inch piece of light brown construction paper
(2) buttons
(1) 3x4-inch piece of wallpaper
(1) 1x4-inch piece of tagboard
Bear pattern
Crayons or marking pens
Scissors
Glue

LET'S BEGIN:

1. Read *Corduroy*.
2. Trace the bear pattern on the light brown paper and cut it out.

3. Draw in facial features.

4. Draw and color overalls for your Corduroy.

5. Glue buttons on the overalls.
6. Read *A Pocket for Corduroy*.
7. Cut a pocket from wallpaper and put glue around three edges. Place the pocket on the overalls.

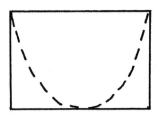

8. Copy "Corduroy" on the narrow strip of tagboard and put your name on the other side.
9. Place the name strip in Corduroy's pocket.

NOTES:

Make this a two-day project.

Children may want to give their bear a new name.

Children will enjoy the movable piece and the real buttons.

Related books about pockets:
    Peter's Pocket, by Judi Barrett

    Katy No-Pocket, by Emmy Payne

    What Can You Do with a Pocket?, by Eve Merriam

Other books by Don Freeman:
    Beady Bear   *Hattie, the Backstage Bat*

    Bearymore   *Quiet—There's a Canary in the Library*

    The Chalk Box Story   *The Seal and the Slick*

    Dandelion

Flat Stanley

Jeff Brown

(Harper & Row, 1964)

Stanley's bulletin board falls during the night and flattens him like a pancake. Flat Stanley begins to enjoy being flat and finds he can slip into an envelope, drop through a street grate, and be flown as a kite.

PURPOSE:

This activity involves creating a flat bookmark representing the events in *Flat Stanley*.

MATERIALS:

(1) 6x6-inch piece of tagboard
Flat Stanley pattern
Scissors
Crayons or marking pens

LET'S BEGIN:

1. Read *Flat Stanley*.
2. Draw around the Flat Stanley pattern on the piece of tagboard.

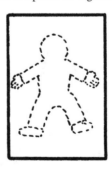

3. Cut out Flat Stanley.
4. With marking pens, draw the front of Stanley on one side.
5. Draw the back view of Stanley on the other side.
6. Enjoy using Flat Stanley as a bookmark with the next book you read.

NOTES:

Some children will like to make a similar bookmark that pictures themselves.

Creative writing activity: What further adventures could Stanley enjoy by being flat?

Make Flat Stanley into a stick puppet.

On large butcher paper, let children outline themselves and color in—now we have life-size "Flat Stanleys."

Children enjoy reading all the Barbapapa stories in which the Barbapapa changes shape. Barbapapa books are by Annette Tison and Talus Taylor.

These bookmarks are nice if laminated.

The Little Red Balloon

Iela Mari

(Barron, 1979)

This is a wordless picture book illustrated in black and white with the addition of the red balloon. The balloon's adventures throughout this book will delight children of all ages.

PURPOSE:

This activity provides each child with a red balloon shape. The children cut the shape in order to add another imaginative adventure to the story.

MATERIALS:

(1) 8½x8½-inch white paper
(1) 7-inch red paper circle
Scissors
Glue
Black crayon or pen

LET'S BEGIN:

1. Read *The Little Red Balloon* several times.
2. Think of several other things the red balloon could become without losing too much of its original shape. Example: a snowflake, a cloud, etc.
3. With one shape in mind, cut your circle to make your new red adventure piece.

4. Glue your new red shape onto the white paper.
5. Add background details with black crayon.
6. Share your results with the class.

NOTES:

The results may be displayed on a bulletin board or put together into a class book.

Cut balloon shapes and write stories about balloons.

If you have access to helium, you could send balloon messages, with the children's names and addresses, up in the sky.

Related books about balloons:
    Balloon Trip, by Ron Wegen

    The Red Balloon, by Albert Lamorisse

Other books written by Iela Mari:
    The Apple and the Moth

    The Chicken and the Egg

    The Tree and the Seasons

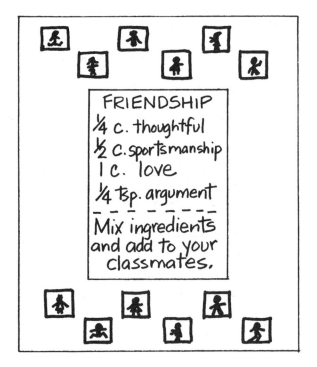

The 329th Friend

Marjorie Weiman Sharmat

(Four Winds, 1979)

Emery Raccoon invites 328 guests for lunch, hoping that someone will be his friend. Emery's preparations and the arrival of his guests are delightful experiences. A very touching incident leads Emery to discover his 329th friend—HIMSELF!

PURPOSE:

This activity provides an opportunity for children to reflect upon the qualities of friendship.

MATERIALS:

(1) 22x28-inch piece of tagboard (lined if available)
(1) 4½x6-inch piece of white paper
Crayons or marking pens

LET'S BEGIN:

1. Read *The 329th Friend*.
2. Discuss as a group general recipes for your favorite foods. Discuss the need for ingredients, measurements, and procedures to achieve good results.
3. Write a group recipe for friendship. Think of specific qualities that are important in a friendship. Try to include some special qualities of your friends.
4. Record the recipe as a group experience story on the tagboard. Example: 1 cup kindness.
5. Draw yourself as a friend on the white paper. Display your picture with the recipe.

NOTES:

This idea will be more successful if you spend time with step 2 rather than beginning by asking for a friendship recipe right away.

A good follow-up is to develop a group recipe for "Parenting" and display it for open house.

Older children can write individual recipes and share them with the class.

You might discuss the qualities we should leave out. Example: jealousy.

Related books:
> *A Friend Can Help*, by Terry Berger
>
> *I'm Glad to Be Me*, by P. K. Hallinan
>
> *People*, by Peter Spier

Marjorie Weiman Sharmat's other books on self-esteem:
> *Lucretia the Unbearable*
>
> *I'm Terrific*
>
> *Thornton the Worrier*

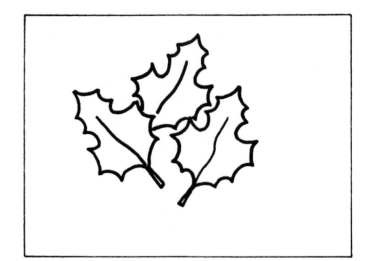

Mr. Tamarin's Trees

Kathryn Ernst

(Crown, 1976)

Mr. Tamarin struggles with nature as his annoyance with autumn and falling leaves provokes him to cut down every tree on his property.

PURPOSE:

This activity extends the story illustration and theme as the children recreate fall leaves for classroom display.

MATERIALS:

White paper (any kind)
Watercolor paints
Pencil
Leaf pattern
Scissors

LET'S BEGIN:

1. Read *Mr. Tamarin's Tree*.
2. Use a watercolor wash on the white paper of autumn colors—brown, orange, yellow, red, and gold.
3. Paint the paper completely, using these colors.
4. Let the paper dry.
5. Trace the leaf pattern on the painted paper.

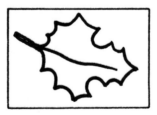

6. Cut out the leaves and use for classroom decoration.

NOTES:

Use this book when studying the seasons.

NOTES:

This activity can also be done successfully by cutting out magazine pictures and pasting them on 5x8-inch cards. Give a card to each child and let them decide what the item in the picture is a "house for"; then have them complete the sentence "A _____ is a house for a _____ , but a house is a house for me."

Example: Using a magazine cut-out picture of a spaceship. The child shows the picture to the group and says, "A *spaceship* is a house for *astronauts*, but a house is a house for me."

Allow for individual children's interpretations. Assist children in following the sentence pattern if needed.

"A _____ is a house for
a _____ , but a house is
a house for me."

cereal bowl   glove
closet   piano
grocery bag   mirror
barn   purse
toaster   cowboy boot
book bag   tent
wastebasket   picture frame
school bus   hat
vacuum cleaner   lunch bag
rocket ship   notebook

The Pumpkin Smasher

Anita Benarde

(Walker & Co., 1972)

This is a Halloween story that is enjoyed during all seasons. The terrible Turner twins trick the pumpkin-smashing witch and save the Halloween spirit in the town of Cranbury.

PURPOSE:

This activity incorporates an art technique while following the theme of the story.

MATERIALS:

(1) 9x12-inch piece of orange paper
(1) 9x12-inch piece of black paper
Crayons or marking pens
Scissors
Glue

LET'S BEGIN:

1. Read *The Pumpkin Smasher*.
2. Make a jack-o'-lantern on the orange paper.
3. Cut the jack-o'-lantern out.
4. Cut the jack-o'-lantern into six pieces.

5. Place the pieces on the black paper, separating them but keeping the general shape of the pumpkin.
6. Glue the pieces in place on the black paper.

NOTES:

Display as a bulletin board of smashed pumpkins along with the title of the book.

Be sure to limit the number of cut pieces to six; otherwise the children will not be able to put the pumpkin shape back together.

Painting rocks to look like jack-o'-lanterns is an enjoyable extension of this book, if suitable rocks are available.

Related pumpkin stories:
The Halloween Pumpkin, by Pamela Oldfield

The Halloween Pumpkin Smasher, by Judith St. George

How Spider Saved Halloween, by Robert Kraus

The Wonderful Pumpkin, by Lennart Hellsing

The Bump in the Night

Anne Rockwell

(Greenwillow, 1979)

Toby the Tinker was not afraid of anything. The ghost in the castle that went BUMP in the night did not scare him away. Instead Toby was able to assemble the ghost by putting together his body pieces as they tumbled down the chimney with a BUMP. The ghost was finally happy and rewarded Toby with bags of silver spoons and gold rings.

PURPOSE:

This activity has children assemble the ghost figure by tinkering with the pattern pieces and brads just like Toby tinkered with them in the story.

MATERIALS:

(1) ghost pattern pieces copied on light construction paper
(3) brads
Scissors
Crayons or marking pens

LET'S BEGIN:

1. Read *The Bump in the Night*.
2. Take the pattern pieces and color them.
3. Cut out the pattern pieces.
4. Connect the head to the body with a brad.

5. Connect the legs to the body with the remaining two brads.
6. Disassemble your ghost and reenact the story by letting the pieces fall to the floor with a BUMP.

NOTES:

Make a chimney out of a shoe box and let the pieces fall out of the chimney.

Read another version of this Spanish folktale in *Feasts and Frolics for Special Days*, selected by Phyliss R. Fenner; "The Tinker and the Ghost," by Ralph S. Boggs and Mary Gould Davis.

Other books by Anne Rockwell:
The Awful Mess
The Girl with a Donkey Tail
The Gollywhopper Egg
Gray Goose and Gander and Other Mother Goose Rhymes
Tuhurahura and the Whale

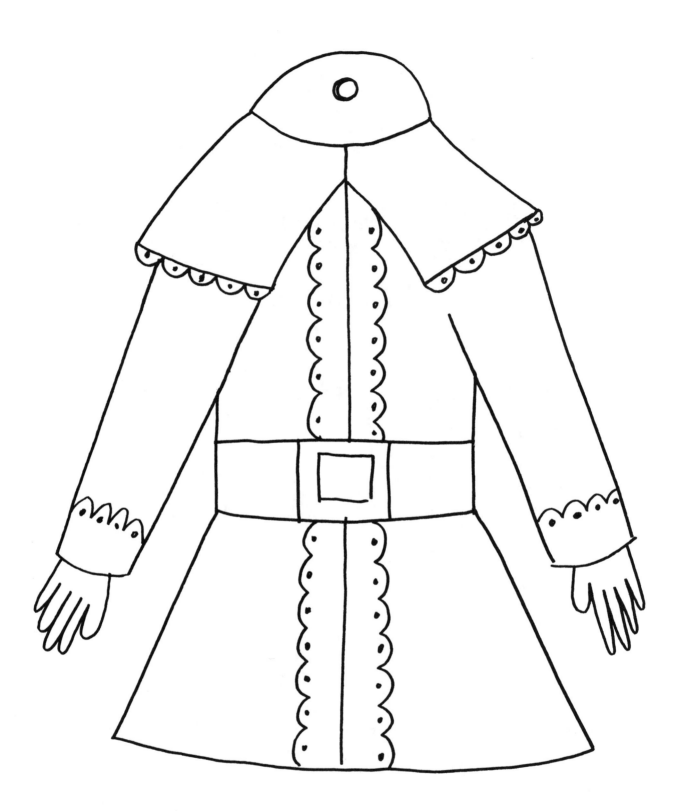

There's an Ant in Anthony

Bernard Most

(Morrow, 1980)

Anthony discovers an "ant" in his own name and begins searching for the "ant" in other words. He searches in the North Pole, the zoo, the city, and all over the globe to collect his jar of "ants."

PURPOSE:

This activity is a literature-related spelling lesson.

MATERIALS:

(1) 12x18-inch piece of white paper
Pencil
Red crayon or marking pen

LET'S BEGIN:

1. Read *There's an Ant in Anthony*.
2. Think of words containing "ant." Make a class list on the chalkboard.
3. Record all the "ant" words you can think of on white paper.
4. Underline the "ant" in each word with red pen.
5. Draw a border of red ants around the edge of the paper, using the inside cover of the book as a sample.
6. To draw the ants:
   a. Draw three circles close together.
   b. Draw two legs on each circle.
   c. Add an eye and two antennae onto the first circle.

NOTES:

Use "ant" words as the basis for your weekly spelling list.

Look for "ant" words as a homework assignment.

Are there any "bugs" or small words in your first or last name?

Play a word game making as many words as possible using the letters in the word "Anthony"—ant, Ann, any, etc.

Use your "ant" words in a sentence or story and illustrate it.

Related books:
　　Henry's Awful Mistake, by Robert Quackenbush
　　I Can't Said the Ant, by Polly Cameron

Some other word game books:
　　CDB, by William Steig
　　A Chocolate Moose for Dinner, by Fred Gwynne
　　The King Who Rained, by Fred Gwynne
　　The Sixteen Hand Horse, by Fred Gwynne

A Perfect Nose for Ralph

Jane Breskin Zalben

(Philomel, 1980)

Reggie's favorite panda, Ralph, has lost his nose. Reggie searches for a perfect nose by trying different objects—from a button to a cherry. Reggie solves the problem in a very loving way, maybe not the perfect way, but the nose looks right on Ralph and that makes it perfect.

PURPOSE:

Each individual can find a "perfect" nose for Ralph by thinking of imaginative objects to place on a patterned panda bear.

MATERIALS:

(1) 9x12-inch piece of white construction paper
Panda pattern
Black crayon
Scissors
Miscellaneous round objects

LET'S BEGIN:

1. Read *A Perfect Nose for Ralph*.
2. Copy the panda pattern onto the white paper.
3. Color the panda appropriately, leaving the nose off.

4. Let each child choose the perfect nose for his/her panda (e.g., button, checker, candy piece, sticker, etc.) and glue into place.
5. Display the pandas with all the "perfect noses" on a large bulletin board.

NOTES:

This project makes a good homework assignment and gives children an opportunity to select an unusual object from home.

Related books:
Ira Sleeps Over, by Bernard Waber

Panda's Puzzle and His Voyage of Discovery, by Michael Foreman

Please Send a Panda, by Ruth Orbach

Some children will copy the ideas from the book, but a lesson on shapes could help them expand their ideas from very simple round objects to more imaginative ones.

Other books by Jane Breskin Zalben:
Norton's Nighttime

Will You Count the Stars without Me?

A Perfect Nose for Ralph

The Maggie B.

Irene Haas

(Atheneum, 1977)

Margaret Barnstable's wish comes true as she and her brother spend a wonderful day sailing on the ship called the Maggie B. It is a most wonderful ship with everything they need, including a little farm on the deck.

PURPOSE:

This activity provides movement and recognition of shapes as children create their own Maggie B.

MATERIALS:

(1) 9x12-inch piece of light blue construction paper
(1) copy of the Maggie B. pattern
Glue
Crayons or marking pens
Scissors

LET'S BEGIN:

1. Read *The Maggie B.*
2. Cut out the shapes of the Maggie B. pattern.
3. Assemble the pieces to design and build your own Maggie B. ship.
4. Glue the pieces on the light blue paper.
5. Add details to the ship and fill in the background with water, waves, sea gulls, etc.

NOTES:

Display as a bulletin board, including the title of the book. Some children may choose not to use all the pieces.

Related books:

"As I Went Over the Water," from *Hector Protector and As I Went Over the Water: Two Nursery Rhymes with Pictures*, by Maurice Sendak

Come Away from the Water, Shirley, by John Burningham

Hurray for Captain Jane, by Sam Reavin

Another book about shapes and recognition of shapes, *The Wing on a Flea*, by Ed Emberley, has been made into a filmstrip.

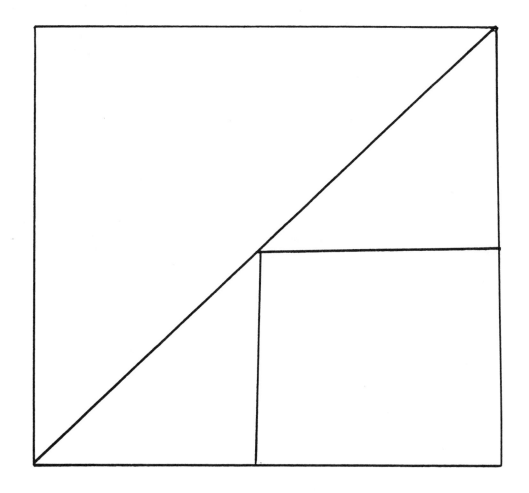

The Bed Just So

Jeanne B. Hardendorff

(Four Winds, 1975)

This is a delightful folktale about a tailor and his search for a hudgin's bed. The hudgin interrupts the tailor's sleep each night with his grumbling until the tailor finds the perfect solution.

PURPOSE:

This activity allows each child to have his or her own imaginary hudgin. Each child uses a walnut shell to reconstruct a bed for his or her hudgin.

MATERIALS:

1/2 walnut shell
Cotton ball
Leaf
Mustard seed or other small seed

LET'S BEGIN:

1. Read *The Bed Just So*.
2. Carefully clean out your walnut shell.
3. Line the bottom of the shell with the cotton ball.
4. Find a leaf to use as a blanket for your walnut-shell bed.
5. Place a mustard seed carefully on the cotton and cover your "hudgin" with the leaf.

NOTES:

This is a good story to reread after the project is completed.

The children will enjoy responding with the hudgin as the tailor searches for the perfect bed. You may want to glue the walnut on a piece of paper in order to provide your hudgin with a rug.

Be prepared to lose lots of hudgins.

Parents could help by sending in walnut halves after holiday baking.

You can substitute cookie sprinkles and quilted material for the mustard seed and leaf.

Santa Makes a Change

Sol Chaneles

(Parents, 1970)

Santa Claus is tired of his familiar red suit with the white fur trim and black boots and belt. He calls together his helpers and the reindeer to help him choose a new outfit. Santa tries on many costumes, appearing as a spaceman, cowboy, railway engineer, and others.

PURPOSE:

This activity involves designing your own original costume for Santa Claus after reading the suggestions in the book.

MATERIALS:

(1) copy of Santa Claus pattern
Crayons or marking pens

LET'S BEGIN:

1. Read *Santa Makes a Change*, showing the pictures of Santa Claus wearing different outfits.
2. On the Santa pattern, design an outfit for Santa Claus to wear. Think of Halloween and the many different costumes people wear. Think of television personalities and book characters you know. Think of props and accessories that go with each costume.
3. Draw the costume with pens or crayons on the copied outline. It is important to tell the children that they may go outside the lines to create the costume.

4. Put the class ideas together in a book titled   Santa Makes More Changes.
5. To make a cover for the book, cover two pieces of cardboard with Christmas wrapping paper. Punch holes in the individual pages and tie together with yarn.

NOTES:

Save the book you made from year to year as inspiration for new ideas.

Related books:
Carol Burnett: What I Want to Be When I Grow Up, by George Mendoza and Sheldon Secunda

Mouse's Terrible Halloween, by True Kelley

Santa's New Suit Funbook, by Beverly Scott

There's a Party at Mona's Tonight, by Harry Allard

A Book of Hugs

Dave Ross

(T. Y. Crowell, 1980)

This is a delightfully illustrated book all about hugs and hugging. All types of hugs are included: animal hugs, people hugs, thing hugs, and special hugs. Helpful hints for hugging are given.

My Homework Hug List

Type of hug	Huggee
bear hug	dad
octopus hug	mom
fraidycat hug	none
people hugs	Chris
hand hugs	me
thing hugs	teddy
special hugs	Grandma

Read A Book of Hugs by David Ross

PURPOSE:

Each child is given the opportunity to give and receive hugs. They learn to appreciate physical affection through a homework assignment.

MATERIALS:

(1) copy of the hug list
Hugger
Huggee
Pencil

LET'S BEGIN:

1. Read *A Book of Hugs*.
2. Discuss hugs: your favorites, your least liked, etc.
3. Take the hug list home for a homework assignment.
4. Think of who and what you will hug at home. Example: your dog, mother, teddy bear, etc.
5. Give your hugs. Receive your hugs.
6. Complete your hug list by writing in the appropriate answers.
7. Return the list to school and share your "hugs."

NOTES:

This is just for fun. Explore the different ways we express caring and affection.

"Free to Be You and Me" is an excellent record expressing caring.

Related books:

A Friend Is Someone Who Likes You, by Joan Walsh Anglund

Good-bye Funny Dumpy Lumpy, by Bernard Waber

Happiness Is a Warm Puppy, by Charles M. Schulz

Love Is a Special Way of Feeling, by Joan Walsh Anglund

No Kiss for Mother, by Tomi Ungerer

Small children may need help completing their list.

Older children can appreciate the cleverness and humor of the book.

A new hug to try is the E. T. Hug.

My Homework Hug List

Type of hug	Huggee (receiver)
bear hug	_____
octopus hug	_____
fraidycat hug	_____
people hugs	_____
hand hugs	_____
thing hugs	_____
special hugs	_____

Read <u>A Book of Hugs</u>
by David Ross

The Christmas Cookie Sprinkle Snitcher

Robert Kraus

(Windmill, 1969)

This delightful Christmas story is written in verse and colorfully illustrated by VIP. Nat is the hero of the story as he tracks down the Christmas Cookie Sprinkle Snitcher.

PURPOSE:

This activity is an amusing reenactment of the ending of *The Christmas Cookie Sprinkle Snitcher*.

MATERIALS:

    (1) plain sugar cookie
    (1) popsicle stick
    (1) small recipe of frosting
    (1) 2 oz. bag of cake/cookie sprinkles

LET'S BEGIN:

1. Read *The Christmas Cookie Sprinkle Snitcher*.
2. Take a plain sugar cookie.
3. Put a teaspoon of frosting on your popsicle stick.
4. Frost your cookie.
5. Take the cookie outside or to an area that is easy to sweep.
6. Stand in a group with your classmates.
7. Hold your cookie up as your teacher sprinkles sprinkles from overhead onto your frosted cookie.
8. Eat and enjoy.

NOTES:

This project can be used as an activity during a Christmas party.

You can substitute paper cookies and sprinkle with glitter or paper confetti.

Children can make cookies from scratch or use refrigerated sugar cookie dough.

Related Christmas cookie books:

Arthur's Christmas Cookies, by Lillian Hoban

The Christmas Cookie Tree, by Ruth Irion

Robert Kraus has written two other Christmas stories:

How Spider Saved Christmas

The Tree That Stayed Up until Next Christmas

Families

Meredith Tax

(Little, Brown, 1981)

This book about families is a lovely look at today's families. Families of all sizes and styles are thoughtfully considered and relationships explored, including animal families. The important conclusion to be drawn from this book is the value of family love.

PURPOSE:

Each child makes an old-fashioned family portrait by portraying the members of his or her family. Following a simple pattern, children add individual characteristics of family members.

MATERIALS:

(1) 9x12-inch piece of black construction paper
(1) white oval pattern
(1) 1/2x2 1/2-inch white strip
Small ovals for each family member
One clothes pattern for each family member
Glue
Scissors
Crayons or marking pens

LET'S BEGIN:

1. Read *Families*.
2. Take as many small ovals as you have family members. Don't forget to include yourself.
3. Place oval heads across the center of your large white oval. You should group them on the bottom two-thirds of the oval, leaving the top part white.

4. For each family member, take a pattern for the clothes. Place a clothes pattern under each small oval.
5. Arrange the pieces carefully and glue them onto the large oval.

6. Add characteristic details to the faces (glasses, hair styles, eye color, jewelry, mustaches, etc.).
7. Design individual outfits with your family member's favorite colors, etc.
8. Trim any overhanging clothing pieces from the large oval.

9. Glue the large oval onto the black paper.
10. Write your family name in black on the small white strip and glue under the large white oval.

NOTES:

These portraits make a nice display for open house.

This is a new way to have children draw their family.

Read *Simple Pictures Are Best*, by Nancy Willard.

Related family books:
> *Feelings between Brothers and Sisters*, by Marcia Conta
>
> *He's My Brother*, by Joe Lasker
>
> *The Nitty Gritty of Family Life*, by Joy Wilt

I'm Terrific

Marjorie Weiman Sharmat

(Scholastic Book Services, 1977)

Jason Everett Bear does terrific things and rewards himself with gold stars. Jason loses his friends in his search for his "terrific" self. He finally discovers a way to be happy with himself and his friends, without the aid of gold stars.

PURPOSE:

This activity encourages children to be happy with themselves and appreciate their individual talents. Parents and teachers are involved in this recognition of self-esteem.

MATERIALS:

(1) 2x9-inch piece of blue construction paper
(1) 4x4-inch piece of yellow construction paper
(3) gold stars
Scissors or pinking shears
Crayons or marking pens
Glue

LET'S BEGIN:

1. Read *I'm Terrific*.
2. Draw a circle on the yellow paper and cut it out with the scissors or pinking shears.

3. Cut out a triangular notch from the bottom of the blue paper.

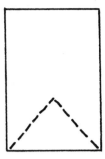

4. Form a badge by gluing the yellow circle to the top of the blue piece.
5. List three terrific things you do and write them on the badge.
6. Earn three gold stars for your badge by sharing your terrific traits with the class.

NOTES:

This is an excellent homework assignment.

You may also make a large classroom badge on which each class member may record his or her specialty.

Have the children tell three terrific things about a partner.

Related books:
 I Know What I Like, by Norma Simon
 I Like to Be Me, by Barbara Bel Geddes

Introduce the children to the world of Marjorie Weiman Sharmat. She has a great understanding of children's insecurities and problems and deals with them in a delightful way.

Some of her other books to enjoy are:
 Burton and Dudley
 Grumley the Grouch
 Lucretia the Unbearable
 Mooch the Messy
 Nate the Great
 Sophie and Gussie
 Thornton the Worrier
 The 329th Friend

The Whingdingdilly

Bill Peet

(Houghton Mifflin, 1970)

Scamp doesn't like being a plain, ordinary dog. He wants to be famous. A witch named Zildy magically turns him into a "whingdingdilly." He is caught and becomes famous. The book has a funny and happy ending, with Scamp finding out that being a plain "ole" dog is best!

PURPOSE:

This activity develops listening skills. The children draw each part of the whingdingdilly as they listen to the story.

MATERIALS:

(1) 9x12-inch piece of drawing paper
Pencil
Crayons or marking pens

LET'S BEGIN:

1. Cover the picture of the whingdingdilly on the book cover with a sheet of paper. Have the children seated at their desks with drawing paper and pencil.
2. Begin reading *The Whingdingdilly*.
3. Read until the first magic spell on the top of page 14. Stop reading.
4. Instruct the children to draw the camel's hump in the center of their drawing paper.

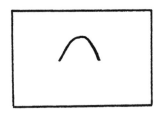

5. Continue reading the next five spells on pages 15, 16, 17, and 18. Be sure to stop after each additional spell and give the children time to draw the animal part. As you go along, do not show the pictures in the book. As the children listen, they will draw the appropriate animal parts on their whingdingdillys.
6. Share individual samples of children's completed whingdingdillys.
7. Show the cover of the book and share Bill Peet's drawing of the whingdingdilly.
8. Finish reading the story.
9. Give the children time to finish their pictures with color.

NOTES:

This is a listening lesson and should be treated as such.

Stress that the whingdingdilly is a make-believe animal; therefore all results are acceptable and entertaining.

Use "If I were a whingdingdilly I would _____" as a story starter.

Related books about mixed-up animals:
    Giraffe and a Half, by Shel Silverstein

    Hit or Myth, by James Riddell

    The Mixed-Up Chameleon, by Eric Carle

    Ookie-Spooky, by Mira Ginsburg

Delightful books written by Bill Peet:
    The Ant and the Elephant

    Big Bad Bruce

    Cowardly Clyde

    Ella

    Hubert's Hair-Raising Adventure

    Jennifer and Josephine

    Kermit the Hermit

    The Wump World

A Color of His Own

Leo Lionni

(Pantheon, 1976)

A chameleon who is tired of changing colors decides to remain on one leaf, but he discovers more problems as the seasons change. He meets another chameleon in the spring, and they change colors together happily ever after.

PURPOSE:

The concept of camouflage in nature is reinforced as animals blend into their natural background for protection. In this project, children make a chameleon and camouflage background out of wallpaper.

MATERIALS:

(2) 9x6-inch pieces of matching patterned wallpaper
(2) 1x3-inch strips of tagboard
(1) 1 cm wiggly eye
Scissors
Stapler
Chameleon pattern

LET'S BEGIN:

1. Read *A Color of His Own*.
2. Trace the pattern of the chameleon onto one sheet of the wallpaper and cut it out.

3. Accordion-fold the two strips of tagboard.

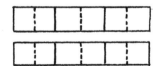

4. Attach the accordion strips to the backside of the chameleon.

5. Attach the other ends of the strips to the matching piece of wallpaper.
6. Glue on the wiggly eye.

NOTES:

Display the results on a large bulletin board, showing all the chameleons camouflaged on their own special backgrounds.

It will be more interesting for each child to have a different wallpaper pattern.

This is a good introduction to learning about animals that camouflage themselves.

Related books:
   Animal Disguises, by Aileen Fisher

   Can You Find the Animal?, by Wilda Ross

Two enjoyable books:
   The Animals Who Changed Their Colors, by Pascale Allamand

   The Mixed Up Chameleon, by Eric Carle

Introduce Leo Lionni as a famous author. Other works by Lionni:
   Alexander and the Wind-Up Mouse

   The Alphabet Tree

   The Biggest House in the World

   Fish Is Fish

   Frederick

   Inch by Inch

   Little Blue and Little Yellow

   Pezzettino

   Swimmy

"Elmer: The Story of a Patchwork Elephant"

from *A Book of Elephants*
compiled by Katie Wales

(Parents, 1977)

Elmer is unhappy because he is not ordinary elephant gray. He doesn't like being different, so he sets out to change his color to gray. When he becomes gray, none of the other elephants recognize him and are very sad. A change of weather saves the day. Each year the elephants have a special Elmer's Day Parade.

PURPOSE:

This activity allows children to decorate their own elephant with patchwork and extend the theme of the book.

MATERIALS:

    (1) copy of the Elmer pattern
    (1) 9x12-inch piece of light construction paper
    (30) 1x1-inch pieces of wrapping paper, wallpaper, or colorful paper
    (1) 2 cm wiggly eye
    Glue
    Scissors

LET'S BEGIN:

    1. Read "Elmer: The Story of a Patchwork Elephant."
    2. Trace the elephant pattern on the construction paper.

    3. Glue the small squares of decorated paper onto the elephant in mosaic fashion. It may be necessary to cut the pieces smaller in some places.

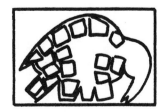

4. Cut the elephant out.
5. Glue the wiggly eye in place.
6. Outline the elephant's ear with a dark crayon.

NOTES:

Display the children's patchwork elephants in an elephant parade led by one plain gray elephant.

Related books:
> *The Animals Who Changed Their Colors*, by Pascale Allamand
>
> *Harlequin and the Gift of Many Colors*, by Remy Charlip
>
> *A Lemon Yellow Elephant Called Trunk*, by Barbara Softly

Other David McKee books:
> *Day the Tide Went Out ... and Out ... and Out ... and Out ... and Out ... and Out*
>
> *Lord Rex: The Lion Who Wished*
>
> *The Man Who Was Going to Mind the House*

Harlequin and the Gift of Many Colors

Remy Charlip

(Parents, 1973)

This is a lovely story of how the Harlequin figure got his costume. Each one of Harlequin's friends gives up a little piece of his or her costume. Out of these pieces, Harlequin's mother makes him a beautiful patchwork costume. At the carnival, Harlequin is happily clothed in the love of his friends.

PURPOSE:

To construct a Harlequin costume on a dance-like figure clothed in patchwork pieces.

MATERIALS:

(1) 9x12-inch piece of white construction paper
(30) pieces of material scraps
Black Crayon
Scissors
Glue

LET'S BEGIN:

1. Read *Harlequin and the Gift of Many Colors*.
2. Make five dots on the white paper, spacing them far apart.

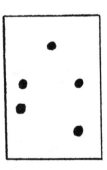

3. Designate one dot for your head.

4. Draw a line from the head to resemble a lollipop stick.

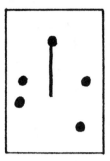

5. Connect the remaining dots to the stick body by making a V to make a bend in the knees and elbows.

6. Glue the scraps on the stick figure to shape the Harlequin costume.
7. When the outfit is completed, add a small oval for his face and design a mask and hat.
8. Add hands and feet or shoes.

NOTES:

This is a more advanced project and children should have time to practice the five-dot action figure on the chalkboard or scratch paper.

This project should be done in two or more sessions.

If possible, obtain pastel scraps of paper or material to complement the pastel illustrations in the book.

Cloth scraps are very effective but more difficult for younger children to work with.

When the finished products are hung side by side on a bulletin board, they present a very effective dance-like image.

Other books by Remy Charlip:
Arm in Arm

Fortunately

Hooray for Me

Mother Mother I Feel Sick Send for the Doctor Quick Quick Quick

Eight Ate a Feast of Homonym Riddles

Marvin Terban

(Clarion, 1982)

The answers to all these silly riddles are combinations of homonyms. Children will enjoy the riddles. Adults will enjoy the concept of homonyms this book of clever riddles teaches.

PURPOSE:

To build awareness of homonyms through clever sentence writing.

MATERIALS:

(1) 6x12-inch piece of white paper
Marking pens or crayons

LET'S BEGIN:

1. Read *Eight Ate a Feast of Homonym Riddles.*
2. Volunteer homonyms for a class list.
3. Choose a set of homonyms. Example: red, read.
4. Using your choice of homonyms, write a sentence on the white sheet of paper.
5. Illustrate your sentence.

NOTES:

Older children can make riddles using the new list of homonyms.

With younger children, a long list of homonyms other than the ones used in the book will motivate new ideas.

The selections can be put together to make a class book of homonyms.

Related books:
> *Homonyms*, by Joan Hanson
>
> *More Homonyms*, by Joan Hanson
>
> *Still More Homonyms*, by Joan Hanson

One Fine Day

Nonny Hogrogian

(Macmillan, 1971)

This cumulative folktale is a Caldecott medal winner. It is based on an Armenian folktale and tells the story of the greedy fox who lapped up the old woman's milk. She became so angry, she chopped off his tail. The words and pictures are fun to follow, making this a good story-hour tale.

PURPOSE:

Children follow each event in this cumulative tale. Each child colors the fox and makes a foxtail. Children then add background details that they remember from listening to the story.

MATERIALS:

    (1) copy of the fox pattern
    (1) 5x3-inch piece of brown construction paper
    Brads
    Crayons or marking pens

LET'S BEGIN:

1. Read *One Fine Day*.
2. Color the fox.
3. Cut the foxtail from the piece of brown paper.

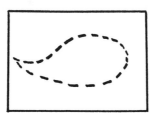

4. Attach the fox tail to the fox with a brad.
5. Add background details which you remember from the story.

NOTES:

Discuss the meaning of "greed." Why is the fox greedy?

Each child will cut the tail individually. Some will be smaller, bushier, and various shapes. Encourage them to use as much of the brown paper as possible for the tail; otherwise the tail may be too small in proportion to the fox. Children may need some assistance in attaching the tail.

Read other cumulative tales as listed in a children's literature anthology.

Related stories:
    The Gingerbread Man, by Paul Galdone

    The King's Tea, by Trinka H. Noble

Other fox stories:
    The Fox Went Out One Chilly Night, by Peter Spier

    Little Fox Goes to the End of the World, by Ann Tompert

    What's in Fox's Sack?, by Paul Galdone

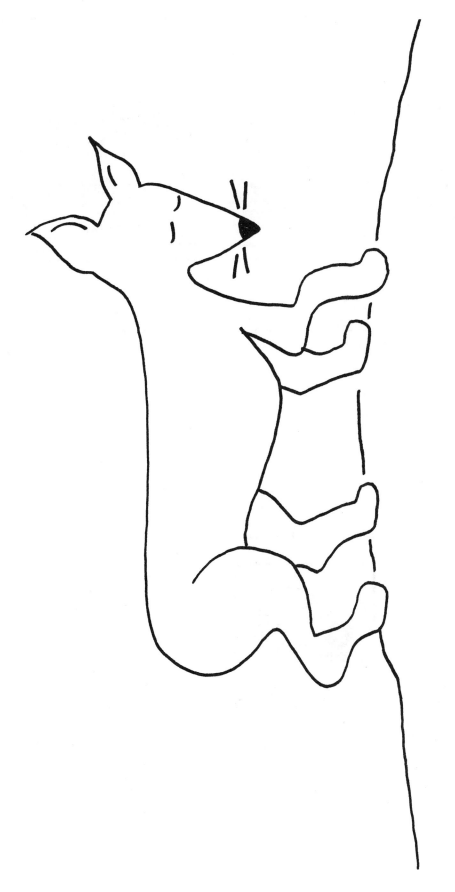

One Fine Day   by Nonny Hogrogian

Tooth-Gnasher Superflash

Daniel Pinkwater

(Four Winds, 1981)

Mr. and Mrs. Popsnorkle and their children test-drive the Tooth-Gnasher Superflash. While pushing the buttons on the dashboard, the Popsnorkles are pleased to see the car turn into different animals. They decide to buy the car.

PURPOSE:

This activity allows children to enjoy an amusing story about cars and gives each child an opportunity to design his own "Superflash," with members of his own family inside.

MATERIALS:

(1) 9x12-inch piece of white drawing paper
(1) 4x4-inch piece of aluminum foil
Crayons or marking pens

LET'S BEGIN:

1. Read *Tooth-Gnasher Superflash*.
2. Design your own "Superflash" car on the piece of white drawing paper.

3. Cut aluminum foil as needed for metallic details such as fenders, chrome, headlights, hubcaps, etc.
4. Draw the members of your family in the car.
5. Choose a "flashy" name for your car.

NOTES:

If possible, show the children pictures of cars prior to starting the drawings of the cars.

Related books:

Classic Sports Cars, by Richard L. Knudson

Drag Racing, by Ed Radlauer

Fabulous Cars of the 1920's and 1930's, by Richard L. Knudson

Hot Rod Mania, by Ruth and Ed Radlauer

Quarter Midget Racing Is for Me, by Mark Lerner

Looking at pictures of cars with the children will result in more details in their drawings.

Children may wish to write an advertisement or commercial for the car they design.

Cut out the cars and mount on black paper to make an attractive bulletin board display.

Related books about cars:

The Green Machine, by Polly Cameron

Mr. Gumpy's Motor Car, by John Burningham

Rodney and Lucinda's Amazing Race, by John Stadler

Tin Lizzie, by Peter Spier

The Yellow Auto Named Ferdinand, by Janosch

The Aminal

Lorna Balian

(Abingdon, 1972)

Patrick was having a picnic when he saw and captured the "aminal." He describes it as round, green, blinky-eyed, with lots of prickly toenails and a waggy tail. Each of his friends imagines the "aminal" and adds details which enhance Patrick's description. When the "aminal" is found, it is ... a turtle.

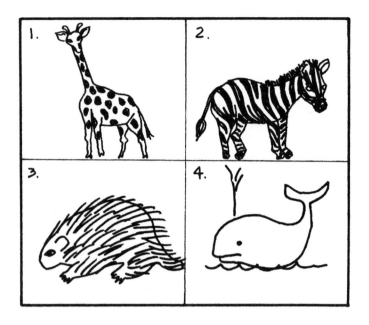

PURPOSE:

This is a listening, imagining, and drawing experience. Each child listens to the description of an animal and draws what he or she hears.

MATERIALS:

(1) 9x12-inch white drawing paper
Crayons or marking pens
Picture book of animals

LET'S BEGIN:

1. Choose several animals the children will know from the animal picture book. Examples: giraffe, zebra, porcupine, whale.
2. Read the story *The Aminal*.
3. Have children fold their white paper into quarters.
4. Number the squares 1-4.
5. Listen carefully to the description of the first animal as given by the teacher. Example: This animal has four legs and a tail. It has two horns and is very quiet. Its body has patch-like brown markings. It lives in Africa. It likes to eat leaves and twigs. It is the tallest of all animals. (The teacher gives clues saving a major clue for the last sentence. While giving clues the teacher is looking at the animal's picture in the animal picture book but does not show the picture to the class.)
6. Now draw the animal your teacher just described in square #1 on your paper.

7. Listen carefully to the description of the next animal. The teacher describes it while looking at the animal book picture. Draw this animal in square #2 on your paper.
8. Follow the same directions for squares #3 and #4 as your teacher describes different animals.
9. Listen to the names of the animals you drew in squares #1, #2, #3, #4. Did you hear all the clues? Which one was the easiest? Which one was the hardest? Look at the pictures of these animals in the animal picture book.

NOTES:

The teacher may describe any four animals for this project, but they should be animals familiar to the children.

Give a strong clue in the last sentence, and build up to this sentence with four or five minor but distinctive clues.

Give the children time to work on their animal drawings after each description (3-5 minutes).

Discuss why Patrick called it an "aminal." Discuss how we sometimes mispronounce words.

Let one of the children describe another animal and have a classmate draw it on the chalkboard.

Discuss listening and why it is important in this lesson to listen carefully to clues. Discuss other situations in which listening is important.

Some good pictorial animal books for the teacher to use are:
The Life Picture Book of Animals, edited by Robert G. Mason

Zoo Babies, by Donn K. Grosvenor

My Very Own Octopus

Bernard Most

(Harcourt Brace Jovanovich, 1980)

A small boy imagines how much fun it would be to have a pet octopus—to play baseball with, to read books with, to trick-or-treat with, to throw snowballs with, etc. The octopus cleverly uses his eight arms to assist the boy in these activities.

PURPOSE:

This activity stimulates children to think of a situation in which an octopus might help them.

MATERIALS:

(1) 12x18-inch piece of white construction paper
(1) 6x4-inch piece of purple construction paper
Crayons or marking pens
Scissors
Glue

LET'S BEGIN:

1. Read *My Very Own Octopus*.
2. Cut a half a circle out of the purple paper. Use the half circle for the body of the octopus.

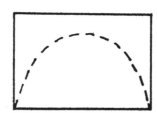

3. Think of an instance in which an octopus might help you. Example: My octopus would help me wash the car.
4. Finish the sentence, "My octopus would help me _____" and write the sentence across the top of your paper.

5. Glue the purple half-circle on the white paper. Add eight purple octopus arms with purple crayon or marking pen. Add octopus eyes and details.

6. Illustrate the sentence you wrote, including your octopus and you in the picture. Be sure your octopus uses all of his arms.

NOTES:

Bernard Most's books are always a story-hour success. See projects in this manual for *If the Dinosaurs Came Back* and *There's an Ant in Anthony*.

Look for factual information about the octopus in an encyclopedia. The *World Book Encyclopedia* has an interesting article. Discuss the terms "fiction" and "nonfiction."

Other octopus stories:

I Was All Thumbs, by Bernard Waber

Herman the Helper, by Robert Kraus

Ocean Mammals, by Sue Beauregard and Jill Fairchild.

Strega Nona

Tomie de Paola

(Prentice-Hall, 1975)

Strega Nona hires Big Anthony to help her care for her house and animals in the Italian town of Cambria. Strega Nona goes on a trip and leaves Big Anthony with her magic cooking pot. Big Anthony's antics and Strega Nona's solution will delight all.

PURPOSE:

This activity involves making a torn paper collage which illustrates the consequences for Big Anthony when the pasta pot keeps cooking and overflows into the village.

MATERIALS:

(1) 5x5-inch piece of black construction paper
(1) 12x18-inch piece of light blue construction paper
(1) 3x3-inch piece of pink/flesh construction paper
(1) 6x6-inch piece of wallpaper or gift wrapping paper
(1) 3x3-inch piece of pastel colored paper
1/2 cup of dry pasta or cereal
Glue
Scissors
Crayons or marking pens

LET'S BEGIN:

1. Read *Strega Nona*.
2. Tear or cut a cooking pot out of the black paper. Glue the pot on the sheet of blue paper.

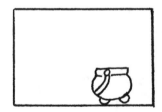

3. Tear or cut Strega Nona's face out of the pink paper, emphasizing the nose and chin features.

4. Cut Strega Nona's dress out of the wallpaper.

5. Glue Strega Nona's face and dress on the large blue paper.

6. Cut a scarf from the pastel paper and glue onto her head.
7. Glue the dry pasta (macaroni, cereal, dried beans) as if it were overflowing from the cooking pot.

8. Add additional details and background, recalling the story and illustrations in the book.

NOTES:

Use this project as part of a folktale unit.

Display all pictures as a bulletin board of Strega Nona collages.

Do another pasta project from the book *Noodle Doodle*, by Karen Mergeler.

Use a pasta machine to demonstrate how homemade pasta is made.

A 16mm film of *Strega Nona* is available from Weston Woods.

Sequels to *Strega Nona*:
    Big Anthony and the Golden Ring
    Strega Nona's Magic Lessons

Related books:
    The Magic Porridge Pot, by Paul Galdone
    The Man Who Entered a Contest, by Phyllis Krasilovsky
    On Top of Spaghetti, by Tom Glazer

Tomie de Paola has written over 100 books for children to enjoy.

Rapunzel

Brothers Grimm

(T. Y. Crowell, 1975)

The witch shut Rapunzel up in a tower deep in the forest on her twelfth birthday. When the prince came to rescue Rapunzel, he climbed up her braid as usual, but instead of Rapunzel, he found the old witch.

PURPOSE:

This activity shows children how to construct the tower with Rapunzel locked inside.

MATERIALS:

(1) 6x18-inch piece of green construction paper
(1) 10x4-inch piece of light brown construction paper
(1) 5-inch triangle of light brown construction paper
(1) 2-inch oval piece of white paper
(3) pieces of yellow yarn 20 inches long
(1) brad
Glue
Crayons or marking pens

LET'S BEGIN:

1. Read *Rapunzel*.
2. Make the tower out of brown construction paper, using the triangle as the roof.
3. Glue the tower on the green paper lengthwise.

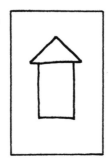

4. Glue the oval near the top of the tower under the roof.
5. Draw a window around the oval.
6. Draw the face of Rapunzel on the oval.
7. Fold the yarn in half, attaching it to the oval with the brad. You should have six strands of yarn to make Rapunzel's ladder of golden hair.

8. Begin braiding the yarn.
   a. Divide the six strands into three groups.
   b. Take the outer left group and pass it over the center group.
   c. Next take the outer right group and pass it over the first one, which is now in the middle.
   d. Continue this process until the braid is finished.
9. Rapunzel's braid may be braided and unbraided repeatedly, or tied off at the end.

NOTES:

Some children will need more help than others in braiding.

Some children will offer to teach others.

To simplify this project, you might use three different colored strands of yarn so each group is a different color.

A heavy book will help weigh down the top of the background paper so the paper does not move while braiding.

Discuss rapunzel and rampion as greens used in a salad.

A variation of the Rapunzel story is *Petrosinella–A Neapolitan Rapunzel*, by Giambattista Basile, adapted from the translation by John Edward Taylor.

There's a Nightmare in My Closet

Mercer Mayer

(Dial, 1968)

A young boy is determined to get rid of the nightmare in his closet. His plan backfires. The outcome will comfort all children who have experienced the fear of a nightmare in their closet.

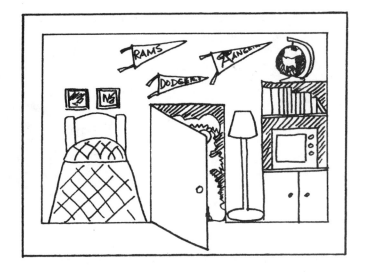

PURPOSE:

This activity provides an opportunity for children to make a picture incorporating the theme of the book and their personal fears.

MATERIALS:

(1) 12x18-inch sheet of white paper (or legal-size typing paper)
Scissors
Glue or stapler
Crayons or marking pens

LET'S BEGIN:

1. Read *There's a Nightmare in My Closet.*
2. Cut the bottom of the paper 3 inches up and 2 inches across. Fold back the cut section to form a door.

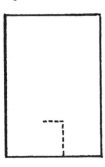

3. Fold the entire paper in half.

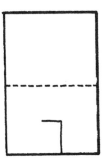

4. Staple or glue the sides together, leaving the door area free.
5. Design a bedroom on the half sheet of paper. Incorporate details and the furniture arrangement from your own bedroom. The door should be your closet door.
6. Open the door and draw a nightmare or monster in the closet.

NOTES:

This activity lends itself easily to a homework assignment and gives children a chance to draw the surroundings of their bedroom.

Younger children may need the paper prepared for them in advance.

Display the finished projects on a bulletin board at the children's eye level.

Encyclopaedia Britannica has a filmstrip series "Monsters and Other Friendly Creatures."

There are many monster and nightmare books written for young children.

Related books:
> *Clyde Monster*, by Robert L. Crowe
>
> *The Gorilla in the Hall*, by Alice Schertle
>
> *In the Night*, by Paul Showers
>
> *Monster Tracks?*, by A. Delaney
>
> *The Monster's Nose Was Cold*, by Joan Hanson
>
> *My Mama Says There Aren't Any Zombies, Ghosts, Vampires, Creatures, Demons, Monsters, Fiends, Goblins or Things*, by Judith Viorst

Other books by Mercer Mayer:
> *Frog Goes to Dinner*
>
> *The Great Cat Chase*
>
> *Just Me and My Dad*
>
> *Little Monster's Library* (a series of six books)
>
> *Professor Wormborg's Search for the Zipperump-A-Zoo*

Owl's New Cards

Kathryn Ernst

(Crown, 1977)

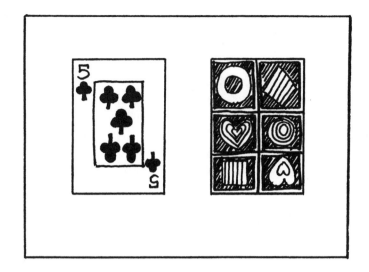

Owl, Brown Bear, and Rat are card-playing buddies. They are upset with the condition of their playing cards, so Owl spends the night making new cards on birchbark while Rat and Bear search for a new deck. The episodes in this book are delightful and sure to bring a smile to all.

PURPOSE:

This activity gives each child a chance to make his or her own playing card and copy some of Owl's ideas.

MATERIALS:

(1) 5x7-inch piece of tagboard
Crayons or marking pens
Samples of playing cards

LET'S BEGIN:

1. Read *Owl's New Cards*.
2. Share samples of different decks of playing cards. Be sure to look at the variety of designs.
3. Use the piece of tagboard and design the back side of the card using the crayons or marking pens.
4. Choose a suit and number. Draw them on the other side of your tagboard.

NOTES:

This activity makes a good homework assignment.

Children less familiar with playing cards will feel more comfortable copying a sample playing card.

Make two or more cards and play memory or a card game with your own rules.

Cards are terrific for teaching math skills.

Related books:
  Card Tricks, by Ken Reisberg
  Let's Play Cards, by John Belton and Joella Cramblit

Kathryn Ernst also wrote *Mr. Tamarin's Trees*.

One-who dances.

Pezzettino

Leo Lionni

(Pantheon, 1975)

Pezzettino means "little piece." This is a story of Pezzettino's search for what or whom he belongs to. A colorful adventure created by Leo Lionni leads Pezzettino to a joyful discovery.

PURPOSE:

This activity has children create an action figure, following the art and language pattern in the book.

MATERIALS:

(1) 8x11-inch piece of one-inch graph paper
(1) 9x12-inch white piece of paper
Marking pens or crayons
Scissors
Glue

LET'S BEGIN:

1. Read *Pezzettino*.
2. Think about the figures Pezzettino meets in the book: the one who runs, the strong one, the swimming one, the one on the mountain, the flying one, and the wise one.
3. Think of another action. Make up a name for your "one who _____" figure. Example: one who dances.
4. Design the figure on the graph paper, filling in the squares with colors to illustrate the characteristics and movement of the figure.

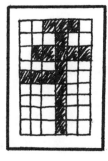

5. Cut the figure out.
6. Glue your figure on the white paper. Write the figure's name on the paper.
7. Share your results with your classmates.

NOTES:

This is a very sophisticated book and older children will get more meaning from Pezzettino's search.

It may be helpful for younger children to choose their favorite sport or action and design a figure for that activity.

Related books:

The Little Circle, by Ann Atwood

The Missing Piece, by Shel Silverstein

The Missing Piece Meets the Big O, by Shel Silverstein

Other books by Leo Lionni:

Alexander and the Wind-Up Mouse

A Color of His Own

Swimmy

My Daddy's Mustache

Naomi Panush Salus

(Doubleday, 1979)

A little boy has never seen his father without a mustache and asks him to shave it off. The father answers that his mustache keeps elephants warm, and the boy imagines walruses, tigers, parrots, penguins, etc., living in Daddy's mustache.

PURPOSE:

Children enjoy the father/son relationship and the fantasy of the father's reply of elephants and other animals living in his mustache. This activity allows each child the fun of wearing a mustache and changing his or her appearance.

MATERIALS:

(1) copy of the mustache pattern
(1) piece of white drawing paper
(1) 3x6-inch piece of black construction paper
Scissors
Marking pens

LET'S BEGIN:

1. Survey the class by asking if fathers, grandfathers, friends wear mustaches. Listen to children's contributions and observations.
2. Read *My Daddy's Mustache*.
3. Trace the mustache pattern onto the black paper.
4. Cut out the mustache.

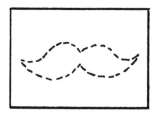

5. Fold the piece of tape back against itself and stick it in the center of the mustache.

6. Gently press the taped mustache on your upper lip.
7. Draw a portrait of yourself with a mustache disguise. Use white paper and marking pens.

NOTES:

Have a mustache day or mustache party. Make a bulletin board of mustache portraits.

Encyclopaedia Britannica filmstrip, "Charlie and the Caterpillar."

My Daddy's Mustache by Naomi Panush Salus

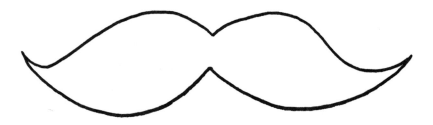

Other styles from The Toy Book by S. Caney

The Field of Buttercups

Alice Boden

(Walck, 1974)

This is a delightful story about Michael O'Grady and the leprechaun he finds. The leprechaun leads Michael to his pot of gold. When Michael returns home for a shovel, the leprechaun tricks him in a very delightful and amusing way.

PURPOSE:

This activity enables a large group of children to make a three-dimensional mural of a field of buttercups for St. Patrick's Day.

MATERIALS:

5-foot length of butcher paper
1-inch squares of yellow tissue paper
Red felt pen
Pencils
Glue

LET'S BEGIN:

1. Read *The Field of Buttercups*.
2. Prepare the butcher paper. Draw a hill across the top third of the paper.

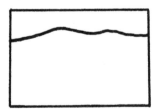

3. Draw as many red 8s as can fill the hill. The red 8s indicate the placement for the yellow tissue paper flowers.

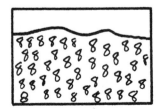

4. To make flowers, place a yellow tissue square on the eraser-tip end of a pencil. Fold the piece carefully over the tip and dip the end in a small amount of glue.

5. Glue each yellow flower on top of each red 8.
6. The yellow flowers on the red 8s will look like red scarves tied around the flower stems.
7. Add details of the sky, Michael O'Grady, the leprechaun, etc.

NOTES:

This is a good St. Patrick's Day project.

You may find it easier to let small groups work on separate sections of the mural.

This is a simple tissue paper art technique which children may be familiar with from previous art lessons.

Other St. Patrick's Day stories:

Leprechauns Never Lie, by Lorna Balian

Munachar and Manachar: An Irish Story as Told by Joseph Jacobs

"Patrick O'Donnel and the Leprechaun," by Virginia Haviland as it appeared in *Cricket Magazine* in March, 1975

apples... hearts... cherry

oranges... pumpkins... carrots

sun... lemons... ducks

frogs... leaves... grapes

sky... pool... ocean

crayon... grapes... violets

flowers... sunset... lipstick

Annie's Rainbow

Ron Brooks

(Philomel, 1976)

Annie thinks a rainbow is the most beautiful thing in the world and tries several ways to get one of her own. During her search, she meets a painter who helps Annie get a rainbow of her own.

PURPOSE:

To enjoy the beauty of rainbow colors by making a tissue paper collage with color word associations.

MATERIALS:

(1) 9x12-inch sheet of white paper
(1) 1½x9-inch strips of red, orange, yellow, green, blue, purple, and magenta tissue paper
Equal parts of glue and water, mixed in a small container
Paintbrush
Black felt pen

LET'S BEGIN:

1. Read *Annie's Rainbow*.
2. Paint glue and water over the entire sheet of white paper.
3. Carefully lay strips of tissue paper side by side. Use the rainbow order of red, orange, yellow, green, blue, purple, and magenta.

Red
Orange
Yellow
Green
Blue
Purple
Magenta

4. With the glue and water, paint over all the strips of colored tissue paper.
5. Allow your tissue-paper rainbow to dry overnight.

6. Think of three word associations for the color of red.
7. Print the three words across the red strip of paper.
8. Follow the same procedure for each color. Think of each color's significance and what it brings to mind.
9. Share your rainbow papers and your color thoughts with your classmates.

NOTES:

This is a two-day assignment.

Reading *Hailstones and Halibut Bones*, by Mary O'Neill, will help evoke new ideas about color associations.

Related books about rainbows:
  Peony's Rainbow, by Martha Weston
  A Rainbow of My Own, by Don Freeman

Older children could write "colorful" poems rather than simple lists of words.

Younger children may need to have an adult write their color words.

Dear Hildegarde

Bernard Waber

(Houghton Mifflin, 1980)

Hildegarde is the "Dear Abby" of the animal world. Whatever problem an animal might have, Hildegarde has something to say about it. Various animals write to her for guidance and direction in dealing with their problems. Hildegarde replies with advice and solutions.

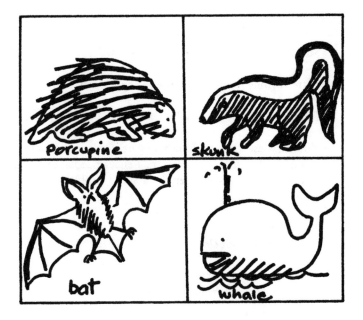

PURPOSE:

Children listen to the problems of the dog, moth, bird, horse, spider, etc., that write to Hildegarde for advice. Following the story, the children compose problem letters to Dear Hildegarde, using the format developed in the book.

MATERIALS:

(1) sheet of notebook paper
(1) envelope
Pencil

LET'S BEGIN:

1. Read *Dear Hildegarde*.
2. Think about some animals not included in the story, e.g., the porcupine, skunk, whale, or bat. You might like to list the various characteristics of these animals.
3. Choose an animal and identify a problem that your animal might have. Write down the problem. Example: Bats spend the day sleeping. Problem: They miss out on all daytime activity. Porcupines have strong, stiff quills. Problem: These quills poke and puncture things around them.
4. After identifying a problem for your animal, compose a letter to "Dear Hildegarde" explaining the details and elaborating on the problem.
5. Put the letter in the envelope and address it to "Dear Hildegarde."

6. The letters can be opened and read aloud or shared with another class.

NOTES:

Some students will be interested in writing replies from Hildegarde to each animal.

Letter writing form can be reviewed and practiced in these letters.

Discussion of the "Dear Abby" column in the newspaper may be a result of the story.

You may use this as a library research assignment and have children do animal research and look up a specific animal in the encyclopedia, animal encyclopedia, or nonfiction animal book. After making a list of characteristics, each child should identify a single problem the animal might have. The attached research sheet may be used.

Related story:
    The Luckiest One of All, by Bill Peet

Other books by Bernard Waber:
    An Anteater Named Arthur

    Good-bye Funny Dumpy-Lumpy

    Ira Sleeps Over

    Lovable Lyle and other Lyle books

    Rich Cat, Poor Cat

Animal Research

Use an encyclopedia, animal encyclopedia, or nonfiction
animal book to list seven characteristics of the animal
you pick.

Your Name _____

Name of Animal _____

List characteristics:

1.

2.

3.

4.

5.

6.

7.

Based on the characteristics you have researched, identify
a problem that your animal might have.
Write the problem.

Problem:

Project: Write a letter to "Dear Hildegarde" pretending you
are an animal with a problem. Describe your problem and the
difficulties you have encountered.

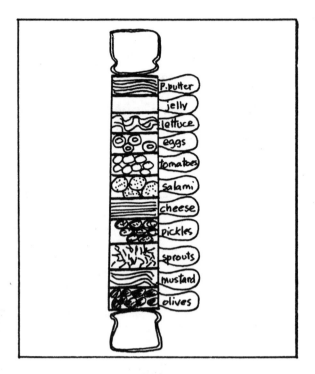

The Biggest Sandwich Ever

Rita Golden Gelman

(Scholastic Book Services, 1980)

While having a picnic, two children are joined by a man who makes the biggest sandwich ever. The pickles are delivered by plane, the ketchup in a firetruck, and the tuna in a dump truck. Children enjoy the exaggeration in the making of the biggest sandwich ever.

PURPOSE:

A group project in which all children can join in making the biggest sandwich ever.

MATERIALS:

(1) copy of the sandwich ingredient pattern
Crayons or marking pens
Pieces of bread (real bread or bread cut from brown construction paper)

LET'S BEGIN:

1. Read *The Biggest Sandwich Ever*.
2. Join in making the biggest "paper" sandwich ever by thinking of an ingredient you might add. Example: cucumbers.
3. Draw and color your sandwich ingredient on the pattern. Label it with your name.

4. Cut out your contribution to the sandwich.
5. Add your sandwich ingredient to the other ingredients made by your classmates.

NOTES:

Make a bulletin board, placing all the sandwich ingredients the children drew between the two pieces of bread. Write a class recipe for the sandwich you made—the biggest sandwich ever.

You might like to have a class party and make an edible sandwich by buying a large loaf of French bread and asking each child to bring one ingredient from home to put inside the sandwich.

Related books:
The Giant Jam Sandwich, by John V. Lord

Sandwichery, by Patricia Stubis

Tunafish Sandwiches, by Patty Wolcott

The Biggest Sandwich Ever
By Rita Gelman

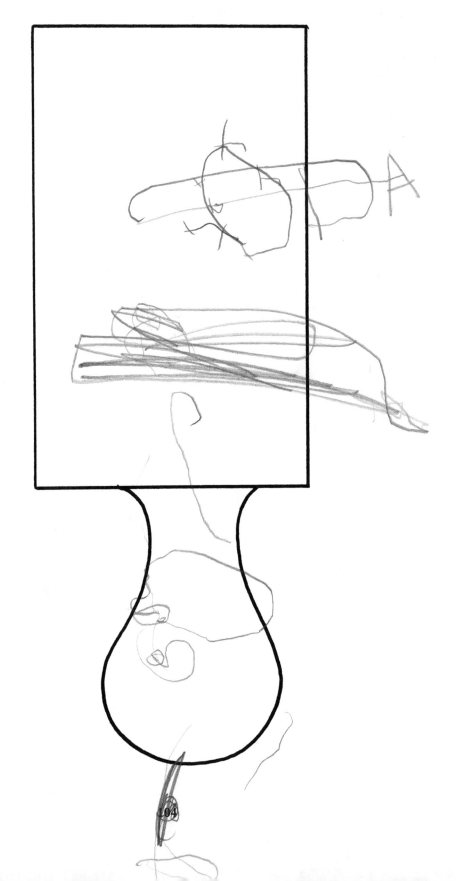

Crictor

Tomi Ungerer

(Harper & Row, 1958)

Crictor, the boa constrictor, attends school with Madame Bodot. Crictor learns to shape the alphabet letters, counts by forming numbers, and enjoys playing with boys and girls. Madame Bodot is attacked by a burglar, but Crictor comes to the rescue.

PURPOSE:

This activity provides tactile experiences. Each child practices forming numbers and letters with a "yarn snake" as Crictor did in the story.

MATERIALS:

(1) 12x18-inch piece of white construction paper
(1) 6-inch piece of green yarn
Glue
Crayons or marking pens

LET'S BEGIN:

1. Read *Crictor*.
2. Pretend the green yarn is Crictor and practice forming the letters of the alphabet and numbers from 1 to 9 on the piece of white paper.
3. Choose one yarn letter that you would like to glue onto the paper permanently.
4. Glue this yarn letter on the paper.

5. Think of words that begin with this letter and list them on your paper following the language pattern in the book.

105

6. Add Crictor's head with eyes and a forked tongue to one end of the piece of yarn.

NOTES:

To make a bulletin board, use the children's work with the title **CRiCTOR** done in snake letters made of yarn.

Another enjoyable school story about a snake is *Mrs. Peloki's Snake*, by Joanne Oppenheim.

Other books by Tomi Ungerer:
The Beast of Monsieur Racine

Moon Man

Rufus

Snail, Where Are You?

Zerelda's Ogre

Enjoy the game of body shapes as part of physical education. The children play this game with one or more partners. Ask if they can make a certain number, shape, or letter with their bodies. How they do it is up to them, just as long as everyone in their group is part of it. For more ideas, see page 12 in *The Cooperative Sports and Games Book*, by Terry Orlick.

The Lonely Skyscraper

Jenny Hawkesworth

(Doubleday, 1980)

A big city skyscraper finds it is lonely when all the workers go home at night. The skyscraper sees the country in the distance and wants to go there. It rocks from side to side and walks to the country where it makes itself a home for forest animals.

PURPOSE:

In this activity, each child, following the story line in the book, builds a skyscraper in the country and fills the windows with forest animals.

MATERIALS:

(1) 12x18-inch white paper
(1) 12x18-inch gray paper
Scissors
Crayons or marking pens
Stapler
Nature magazines such as *Ranger Rick* or *World*

LET'S BEGIN:

1. Read *The Lonely Skyscraper*.
2. Place the gray paper lengthwise and cut a tall skyscraper from it.

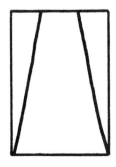

107

3. Draw rows of windows on each floor of the skyscraper. Make each window about two inches wide.
4. Make one large window near the top for the "housewarming party" picture.

5. Cut open some of the windows by cutting around three sides of the window shape to open each window by folding it up.

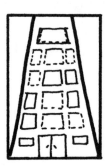

6. Staple the skyscraper onto the white background paper.
7. Open the windows and draw forest animals in each window. (If you do not wish to draw them all, you can cut animal pictures from magazines to fit into the window space.)
8. In the large, narrow window near the top, draw the food for the housewarming party and the animals. Write "housewarming party" on the window flap.
9. Fill in the background so it looks like your skyscraper has moved to the country. Example: grass, trees, mountains, sun, clouds, etc.

NOTES:

Discuss the meaning of a "housewarming party."

Make a list of forest animals on the chalkboard for all to refer to when drawing animals to put in the skyscrapers.

This book can be used with a unit on the city as it nicely contrasts the city and rural environments.

Related books:
  Country Cat, City Cat, by David Kherdian

  Dinosaurs Housewarming Party, by Norma Klein

  Little House, by Virginia L. Burton

  The Skyscraper Book, by James Giblin

SIDE ONE · ABOVE GROUND

SIDE TWO · INSIDE BURROW

Humbug Rabbit

Lorna Balian

(Abingdon, 1974)

The rabbit children believe their father is the Easter Bunny. He says the idea is absurd because rabbits do not lay eggs. Barnaby the cat pushes all the colored eggs into the rabbits' burrow, where they are discovered on Easter morning. The eggs begin hatching, and Father Rabbit begins to wonder if he really is the Easter Bunny.

PURPOSE:

Humbug Rabbit is a simple pictorial introduction to burrowing animals. In an original two-sided picture, the children create the space above ground and the burrow underground.

MATERIALS:

(1) 12x18-inch piece of yellow construction paper
(1) copy of the egg pattern
Scissors
Crayons or marking pens

LET'S BEGIN:

1. Read *Humbug Rabbit*.
2. Discuss the word "burrow." Notice how the author drew the activities inside the burrow at the bottom of each page.
3. On the bottom left side of the yellow paper, trace and cut out the egg pattern.

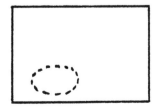

4. On the front side of the paper, draw the outside of the rabbits' burrow, or what is above the ground.

5. Put your hand through the hole, turning the paper over as you do so.

6. On the back side, draw the underground scene of the rabbits' burrow. Use your imagination.

NOTES:

For younger children, or to save time, the egg shape (step 3) may be cut ahead of time.

This project should be done in two activity periods, one for each side of the paper.

Discuss other animals that burrow underground (chipmunk, gopher, prairie dog, spider, etc.).

Related books about burrowing animals:
Animals Build Amazing Homes, by Hedda Nussbaum

Animals That Burrow, by Dean Morris

Mister Mole, by Luis Murschetz

Other holiday books by Lorna Balian:
Bah! Humbug

Humbug Witch

Leprechauns Never Lie

Sometimes It's Turkey, Sometimes It's Feathers

A Sweetheart for Valentine

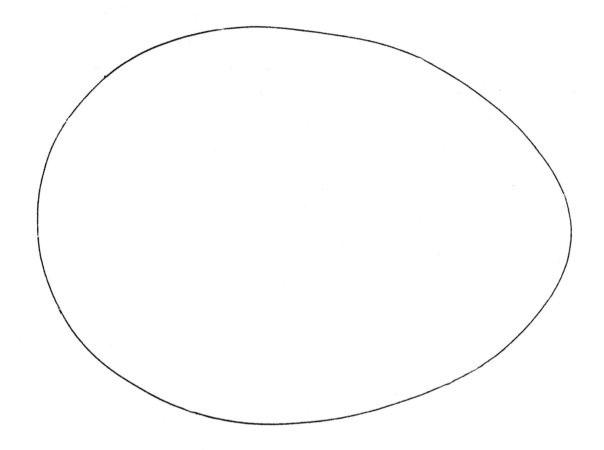

Benjamin's 365 Birthdays

Judi Barrett

(Atheneum, 1974)

Benjamin celebrates his ninth birthday with his friends and presents. He loves the presents so much he decides to celebrate his birthday every day for one year by giving presents to himself.

PURPOSE:

This activity is designed to involve all children in a delightful birthday idea and sharing experience. It is a project for every child who has wished that his or her birthday were every day.

MATERIALS:

One favorite thing to share
Wrapping paper
Ribbon
Tape

LET'S BEGIN:

1. Read *Benjamin's 365 Birthdays*.
2. For homework, you are to choose one favorite thing to share with your class.
3. Gift wrap your choice as a present to yourself just like Benjamin did in the story.
4. Bring your present to school and leave it in the room until share time.
5. During share time, give the class three hints about your gift. Ask three volunteers to guess what your gift is.
6. Unwrap your gift and share it with the group.

NOTES:

Children will enjoy the opportunity of gift wrapping without parental assistance.

This is a good book for introducing the number of days in a year.

Be certain you stress this is to be something the children have at home so no one feels the need to buy something new.

Related books about birthdays:

A Birthday for Frances, by Russell Hoban

Mr. Elephant's Birthday, by Jack Kent

Happy Birthday, Sam, by Pat Hutchins

Other books by Judi Barrett:

Animals Should Definitely Not Wear Clothing

Cloudy with a Chance of Meatballs

Peter's Pocket

The Wind Thief

Look Again

Tana Hoban

(Macmillan, 1971)

This is a photographic picture book of shapes, textures, patterns, and designs with a "see-through" window showing only part of the object. By turning the page and looking again, you can see the entire object.

PURPOSE:

This activity involves surprising others by selecting a magazine photograph for a self-made "look again" picture which follows the format of Tana Hoban's book.

MATERIALS:

(1) 9x8-inch piece of black construction paper
(1) 9x8-inch piece of white paper
Several old magazines (nature magazines are best)
Glue
Scissors
Black pen
Stapler

LET'S BEGIN:

1. Present the book *Look Again* as a guessing game called "look again." Flip the page to show the entire photograph, saying, "Look again," as you turn the page.
2. Give each child time to look through magazine pictures for a good "look again" picture. Children will want to try several selections.
3. Cut a two-inch square out of the center of the white paper.

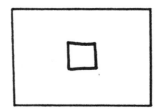

4. Place the magazine pictures on the black paper and cover with the white piece.

5. Staple the white paper to the top of the black paper by putting three staples at the top.

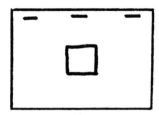

6. Let each child try several pictures in his or her "look again" window, trimming and cutting each picture to fit.
7. Make a final selection and glue it onto the black paper.
8. Print the title *Look Again* and the child's name on the front of the white paper.

NOTES:

For display, these "look again" pictures should be hung at eye level so the children can guess, lift the white paper, and look again.

Other books with photographic illustrations:

Alfred Goes Flying, by Bill Binzen

Big Ones, Little Ones, by Tana Hoban

Is It Red? Is It Yellow? Is It Blue?, by Tana Hoban

One Little Kitten, by Tana Hoban

Push Pull, Empty Full: A Book of Opposites, by Tana Hoban

The Red Balloon, by Albert Lamorisse

Take Another Look, by Tana Hoban

True or False?, by Patricia Ruben

Red Riding Hood: Retold in Verse for Boys and Girls to Read Themselves

Beatrice Schenk de Regniers

(Atheneum, 1973)

This is our favorite version of Little Red Riding Hood. The story is based upon the Grimm Brothers' version but is told in verse. The drawings in the book are done in muted colors and highlighted with bright touches of red.

PURPOSE:

This activity involves creating and manipulating a flip puppet made with the characters from *Red Riding Hood*.

MATERIALS:

(1) 2x6-inch piece of tagboard
(1) facial tissue
Stapler
Crayons or marking pens

LET'S BEGIN:

1. Read *Red Riding Hood*.
2. On the strip of tagboard, measure off three inches and draw a dotted line.

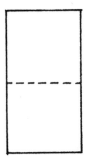

3. Draw a solid line through the center of each half.

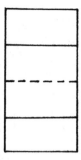

4. Draw Red Riding Hood's face at one end and color the bottom half red.

5. Draw the grandmother at the other end and design grandmother's dress in blue.

6. Flip the doll over and draw the wolf on this side.

7. On the Red Riding Hood side, staple one of the longer sides of the facial tissue to the dotted line in the center of the puppet to form a skirt.

8. When you turn the puppet upside down, the tissue should fall to the opposite side, revealing Red Riding Hood and hiding Grandmother under the tissue.
9. You will need to turn the puppet over to reveal the wicked wolf.

NOTES:

As you retell the story, flip the doll to show Red Riding Hood, her Grandmother, and the wolf.

You can introduce other versions of Little Red Riding Hood. For younger children, the teacher may want to prepare steps 2 and 3 beforehand.

Some children may devise a way to include the woodcutter on the half with the wolf.

Other wolf stories:
    Clever Polly and the Stupid Wolf, by Catherine Storr

    Granny, the Baby and the Big Gray Thing, by Peggy Parish

    It's So Nice to Have a Wolf around the House, by Harry Allard

    Lambs for Dinner, by Betsy Maestro

    Walter the Wolf, by Marjorie Sharmat

A cloth Red Riding Hood flip doll can be made by using Butterick Pattern #4150.

Would You Rather

John Burningham

(T. Y. Crowell, 1978)

This book presents choices for the reader or storytelling audience. The choices are illustrated on each page presenting unusual and amusing dilemmas.

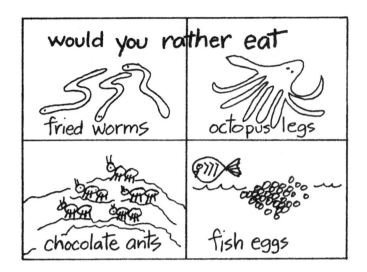

PURPOSE:

This activity is a listening experience as each child listens to the choices and chooses the one alternative he or she would prefer. In a group situation, children can raise their hands to show their choices.

MATERIALS:

(1) 9x12-inch white drawing paper
Crayons or marking pens

LET'S BEGIN:

1. Read *Would You Rather*. While reading the story, stop to allow the children to participate in the individual choices.
2. Fold your paper in quarters. Number each square.
3. On the chalkboard, write some "would you rather" starter sentences, such as:

    Would you rather have _____

    Would you rather eat _____

    Would you rather escape from _____

    Would you rather be _____

    Would you rather live with _____

4. Write one "would you rather" starter sentence across the top of the paper.

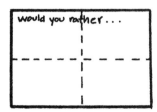

5. In each of the squares, invent an alternative for your "would you rather" sentence.
6. Illustrate your alternatives in each square.
7. Share your ideas with the rest of the group.

NOTES:

Some other story-hour books by John Burningham:
  Cannonball Simp

  Come Away from the Water, Shirley

  The Shopping Basket

The Seamstress of Salzburg

Anita Lobel

(Harper & Row, 1970)

This is the story of a poor girl named Anna who is asked to sew and embroider dresses for all the ladies in Salzburg. Finally, the Queen asks for a special dress as the prince is coming home. Anna is overworked and all the dresses fall apart. The kind prince rescues Anna. Anna offers to teach the ladies in Salzburg how to sew their own dresses.

PURPOSE:

Each child follows Anna's example in the story and designs a beautiful dress embroidered and decorated with ribbon, buttons, and flowers.

MATERIALS:

(1) copy of the dress pattern
Crayons or marking pens
Any decorative materials, such as scraps of ribbon, buttons, sequins, glitter, etc.
Glue

LET'S BEGIN:

1. Read the story *The Seamstress of Salzburg*.
2. Talk about how hard Anna worked on the dresses and notice the decorative details, such as ribbons and bows, decorative borders, flowers, embroidery, etc., in the illustrations.
3. Design and decorate a dress using the pattern outline. Work with marking pens or crayons first and glue on decorative touches last.
4. Cut out the dress you designed.

NOTES:

Boys as well as girls respond positively to this designing project.

Display all the dresses designed by children on a bulletin board.

This project can be accompanied by a simple sewing or embroidery project.

A similar project can be done with the traditional story of *Cinderella* as children design a gown for Cinderella to wear to the ball.

Other books by Anita Lobel:
A Birthday for the Princess
On Market Street

The Ice Cream Cone Coot and Other Rare Birds

Arnold Lobel

(Parents, 1971)

The author has written a rhyming story about very strange and rare birds. The Ice Cream Cone Coot, the Dollarbill Dodo, and the Garbage Canary are a few of the rare birds you will meet in this book.

PURPOSE:

Lobel turns everyday articles into fanciful birds. This collage project takes simple pictures from magazines and develops them further into examples of "rare" birds.

MATERIALS:

(1) 9x12-inch piece of white construction paper
(1) colored feather
Several old magazines
Scissors
Glue
Crayons or marking pens

LET'S BEGIN:

1. Read *The Ice Cream Cone Coot and Other Rare Birds.*
2. Look through magazines for a picture you would like to turn into a special bird.
3. Cut the picture out and glue it onto the white paper.

4. Add a beak, an eye, and feet.

5. Glue a feather onto your bird.
6. Add some background if you wish.
7. Give your bird a new and fanciful name.

NOTES:

Fluffy feathers are available at most craft stores or in craft catalogs.

Use real feathers you have found or collected.

Display the results as a bulletin board of flying fantasies.

Related books:
    A Giraffe and a Half, by Shel Silverstein
    The Nickle Nackle Tree, by Lynley Dodd

Arnold Lobel has written many popular books for children. Some you might introduce are:
    Days with Frog and Toad (a series)
    Giant John
    The Great Blueness and Other Predicaments
    Mouse Soup
    Mouse Tails
    On the Day Peter Stuyvesant Sailed into Town
    A Treeful of Pigs

True or False?

Patricia Ruben

(J. B. Lippincott, 1978)

This book contains black-and-white photographs with simple statements underneath asking if the action in the picture is true or false.

PURPOSE:

By using the format in the book, children can make their own true or false pictures and statements.

MATERIALS:

(1) 9x12-inch sheet of white paper
Several old magazines
Scissors
Glue
Pencil

LET'S BEGIN:

1. Read *True or False?* You may want to read it several times so the children get the feeling for the true-and-false statements.
2. Select two magazine pictures and cut them out carefully.
3. Glue your pictures on the white paper.

4. Make up a true sentence for one of the pictures and a false sentence for the other picture, following the sentence pattern from the book.
5. Write your sentences next to your pictures.
6. Share your results and ask, "Is it true or false?"

NOTES:

Compare this book with those written by Tana Hoban:
>   *Look Again*
>   *Take Another Look*

This is a great way to teach questions.

This is also a good readiness activity for testing procedures.

The individual children's work may be combined and made into a class book.

Two other books written by Patricia Ruben:
>   *Apples to Zippers: An Alphabet Book*
>   *What Is New? What Is Missing? What Is Different?*

You will also enjoy the new book *Puniddles*, by Bruce and Brett McMillan.

Bibliography

Allamand, Pascale — *The Animals Who Changed Their Colors*. Lothrop, 1979.

Allard, Harry — *It's So Nice to Have a Wolf around the House*. Doubleday, 1979. (p.b.)
There's a Party at Mona's Tonight. Doubleday, 1981.

Anglund, Joan Walsh — *A Friend Is Someone Who Likes You*. Harcourt Brace Jovanovich, 1958.
Love Is a Special Way of Feeling. Harcourt Brace Jovanovich, 1960.

Anno, Mitsumasa — *Anno's Alphabet: An Alphabet in Imagination*. T. Y. Crowell, 1975.
Anno's Counting Book. T. Y. Crowell, 1977.
Anno's Journey. Philomel, 1978.

Atwood, Ann — *Little Circle*. Scribner, 1967.

Balian, Lorna — *Bah! Humbug*. Abingdon, 1977.
Humbug Witch. Abingdon, 1965.
Leprechauns Never Lie. Abingdon, 1980.
Sometimes It's Turkey, Sometimes It's Feathers. Abingdon, 1973.
A Sweetheart for Valentine. Abingdon, 1979.

Barlowe, Dot — *Who Lives Here?* Random, 1978.

Barrett, Judi — *Animals Should Definitely Not Wear Clothing*. Atheneum, 1970. (p.b.)
Cloudy with a Chance of Meatballs. Atheneum, 1978.
Peter's Pocket. Atheneum, 1974.
The Wind Thief. Atheneum, 1977.

Basile, Giambattista — *Petrosinella*. Warne, 1981.

Beauregard, Sue, and Jill Fairchild — *Ocean Mammals*. Children's Book Company, 1982.

Bel Geddes, Barbara — *I Like to Be Me*. Young Readers Press, 1963. (p.b.)

Belton, John, and Joella Cramblit — *Let's Play Cards*. Raintree, 1975.

Berger, Terry — *A Friend Can Help*. Raintree, 1974.

Binzen, Bill — *Alfred Goes Flying*. Doubleday, 1976.

Borden, Beatrice Brown	*Wild Animals of Africa*. Random House, 1982.
Burnett, Carol	*What I Want to Be When I Grow Up*. Simon & Schuster, 1975.
Burningham, John	*Cannonball Simp*. T. Y. Crowell, 1977.
	Come Away from the Water, Shirley. T. Y. Crowell, 1977.
	Mr. Gumpy's Motor Car. T. Y. Crowell, 1976. (p.b.)
	Shopping Basket. Harper & Row, 1980.
Burton, Virginia Lee	*The Little House*. Houghton Mifflin, 1957. (p.b.)
Cameron, Polly	*I Can't Said the Ant*. Coward, 1961.
	The Green Machine. Coward, 1969.
Carle, Eric	*The Mixed-up Chameleon*. T. Y. Crowell, 1975.
Charlip, Remy	*Arm in Arm*. Four Winds, 1980.
	Fortunately. Four Winds, 1980.
Charlip, Remy, and Lillian Moore	*Hooray for Me*. Four Winds, 1980.
Charlip, Remy, and Burton Supree	*Harlequin and the Gift of Many Colors*. Four Winds, 1973.
	Mother Mother I Feel Sick Send for the Doctor Quick Quick Quick. Four Winds, 1980.
Conta, Marcia, and Maureen Reardon	*Feelings between Brothers and Sisters*. Raintree, 1974.
Cooper, Elizabeth	*Fish from Japan*. Harcourt Brace Jovanovich, 1969.
Crowe, Robert	*Clyde Monster*. Dutton, 1976.
Delaney, A.	*Monster Tracks?*, Harper & Row, 1981.
de Paola, Tomie	*Big Anthony and the Magic Ring*. Harcourt Brace Jovanovich, 1979.
	Strega Nona's Magic Lessons. Harcourt Brace Jovanovich, , 1982.
Dodd, Lynley	*The Nickle Nackle Tree*. Macmillan, 1978.
Emberley, Ed	*The Wing on a Flea: A Book about Shapes*. Little, Brown, 1961.
Ernst, Kathryn	*Mr. Tamarin's Trees*. Crown, 1976.
	Owl's New Cards. Crown, 1977.
Fenner, Phyllis	*Feasts and Frolics: Special Stories for Special Days*. Knopf, 1949.
Fisher, Aileen	*Animal Disguises*. Bowmar-Noble, 1973.
Foreman, Michael	*Panda's Puzzle and His Voyage of Discovery*. Bradbury, 1978.

Freeman, Don	*Beady Bear*. Viking, 1954.
	Bearymore. Viking, 1976. (p.b.)
	The Chalk Box Story. Harper & Row, 1976.
	Dandelion. Viking, 1964. (p.b.)
	Hattie, the Backstage Bat. Viking, 1970. (p.b.)
	Quiet—There's a Canary in the Library. Childrens, 1969.
	A Rainbow of My Own. Viking, 1966. (p.b.)
	The Seal and the Slick. Viking, 1974.
Galdone, Paul	*The Gingerbread Boy*. Houghton Mifflin, 1975.
	The Magic Porridge Pot. Houghton Mifflin, 1976.
	What's in Fox's Sack? Clarion, 1982.
Giblin, James	*The Skyscraper Book*. Harper & Row, 1981.
Ginsburg, Mira	*Ookie-Spooky*. Crown, 1979.
Glazer, Tom	*On Top of Spaghetti*. Grosset-Dunlap, 1966.
Grimm, Brothers	*Rapunzel: A Tale by the Brothers Grimm*. Harper & Row, 1975.
Grosvenor, Donna K.	*Zoo Babies*. National Geographic, 1978.
Gwynne, Fred	*A Chocolate Moose for Dinner*. Messner, 1981. (p.b.)
	The King Who Rained. Messner, 1981. (p.b.)
	The Sixteen Hand Horse. Windmill, 1980.
Hallinan, P. K.	*I'm Glad to Be Me*. Childrens, 1977.
Hamsa, Bobbie	*Your Pet Bear*. Childrens, 1980.
	Your Pet Camel. Childrens, 1980.
	Your Pet Elephant. Childrens, 1980.
	Your Pet Kangaroo. Childrens, 1980.
	Your Pet Penguin. Childrens, 1980.
Hanson, Joan	*Homonyms*. Lerner, 1972.
	The Monster's Nose Was Cold. Carolrhoda Books, 1971.
	More Homonyms. Lerner, 1973.
	Still More Homonyms. Lerner, 1976.
Hellsing, Lennart	*The Wonderful Pumpkin*. Atheneum, 1975.
Hirsh, Marilyn	*How the World Got Its Color*. Crown, 1972.
Hoban, Lillian	*Arthur's Christmas Cookies*. Harper & Row, 1972.

Hoban, Russell	*A Birthday for Frances.* Harper & Row, 1968.
Hoban, Tana	*Big Ones, Little Ones.* Greenwillow, 1976.
	Is It Red? Is It Yellow? Is It Blue? Greenwillow, 1978.
	One Little Kitten. Greenwillow, 1979.
	Push Pull, Empty Full: A Book of Opposites. Macmillan, 1972. (p.b.)
	Take Another Look. Greenwillow, 1981.
Hutchins, Pat	*Happy Birthday, Sam.* Greenwillow, 1978.
Irion, Ruth	*The Christmas Cookie Tree.* Westminster, 1976.
Jacobs, Joseph	*Munachar and Manachar: An Irish Story as Told by Joseph Jacobs.* Crowell, 1970.
Janosch	*The Yellow Auto Named Ferdinand.* Carolrhoda Books, 1973.
Johnson, Crockett	*Harold and the Purple Crayon.* Harper & Row, 1958.
	Harold's ABC. Harper & Row, 1981.
	Harold's Circus. Harper & Row, 1981.
	Harold's Trip to the Sky. Harper & Row, 1981.
	A Picture for Harold's Room. School Book Services, 1974.
Kelley, True	*Mouse's Terrible Halloween.* Lothrop, 1980.
Kent, Jack	*Mr. Elephant's Birthday Party.* Houghton Mifflin, 1969.
Kherdian, David	*Country Cat, City Cat.* Four Winds, 1978.
Klein, Norma	*Dinosaur's Housewarming Party.* Crown, 1974.
Knight, Vic	*The Night the Crayons Talked.* Borden, 1974.
Knudson, Richard L.	*Classic Sports Cars.* Lerner, 1978.
	Fabulous Cars of the 1920's and 1930's. Lerner, 1981.
Krasilovsky, Phyllis	*The Man Who Entered a Contest.* Doubleday, 1980.
Kraus, Robert	*Herman the Helper.* Windmill, 1981. (p.b.)
	How Spider Saved Christmas. Windmill, 1980.
	The Tree That Stayed Up until Next Christmas. Windmill, 1981. (p.b.)
Lamorisse, Albert	*The Red Balloon.* Doubleday, 1978. (p.b.)
Lasker, Joe	*He's My Brother.* A. Whitman, 1974.
Lerner, Mark	*Quarter Midget Racing Is for Me.* Lerner, 1981.
Lionni, Leo	*Alexander and the Wind-up Mouse.* Pantheon, 1969.
	The Alphabet Tree. Pantheon, 1968.
	The Biggest House in the World. Pantheon, 1968.

Lionni, Leo (contd)	*A Color of His Own*. Pantheon, 1976.
	Fish Is Fish. Pantheon, 1970.
	Frederick. Pantheon, 1966.
	Inch by Inch. Astor-Honor, 1962.
	Little Blue and Little Yellow. Astor-Honor, 1959.
	Pezzettino. Pantheon, 1975.
	Swimmy. Pantheon, 1963. (p.b.)
Lobel, Anita	*A Birthday for the Princess*. Harper & Row, 1973.
	On Market Street. Greenwillow, 1981.
Lobel, Arnold	*Days with Frog and Toad*. Harper & Row, 1979.
	Giant John. Harper & Row, 1964.
	Great Blueness and Other Predicaments. Harper & Row, 1968.
	Mouse Soup. Harper & Row, 1977.
	Mouse Tales. Harper & Row, 1978.
	On Market Street. Greenwillow, 1981.
	On the Day Peter Stuyvesant Sailed into Town. Harper & Row, 1971.
	A Treeful of Pigs. Greenwillow, 1979.
Lord, John V.	*The Giant Jam Sandwich*. Houghton Mifflin, 1973.
Maestro, Betsy	*Lambs for Dinner*. Crown, 1978.
Mann, Peggy	*The Boy with a Billion Pets*. Coward, 1968.
Mari, Iela	*The Tree and the Seasons*. Barron, 1979.
Mari, Iela, and Enzo Mari	*The Apple and the Moth*. Pantheon, 1970.
	The Chicken and the Egg. Pantheon, 1970.
Mason, George	*Animal Homes*. Morrow, 1967.
Mason, Robert G. (ed.)	*The Life Picture Book of Animals*. Time-Life, 1969.
Mayer, Mercer	*Frog Goes to Dinner*. Dial, 1977. (p.b.)
	The Great Cat Chase. Four Winds, 1975. (p.b.)
	Just Me and My Dad. Western, 1977. (p.b.)
	Mercer Mayer's Little Monster's Library. Western, 1978.
	Professor Wormbug in Search for the Zipperump-a-Zoo. Western, 1976.
McKee, David	*Day the Tide Went Out ... and Out ... and Out ... and Out ... and Out ... and Out*. Abelard, 1976.
	Lord Rex: The Lion Who Wished. Abelard, 1973.
	The Man Who Was Going to Mind the House. Abelard, 1973.

McMillan, Bruce and Brett	*Puniddles*. Houghton Mifflin, 1982.
Merriam, Eve	*What Can You Do with a Pocket?* Knopf, 1964.
Morris, Dean	*Animals That Burrow*. Raintree, 1977.
Most, Bernard	*My Very Own Octopus*. Harcourt Brace Jovanovich, 1980. *There's An Ant in Anthony*. Morrow, 1980. *There's An Ape in the Drape*. Morrow, 1980.
Murschetz, Luis	*Mister Mole*. Prentice-Hall, 1976.
Nikly, Michelle	*The Princess on the Nut: Or The Curious Courtship of the Son of the Princess on the Pea*. Faber & Faber, 1981.
Noble, Trinka	*The King's Tea*. Dial, 1979.
Nussbaum, Hedda	*Animals Build Amazing Homes*. Random, 1979.
Oldfield, Pamela	*The Halloween Pumpkin*. Childrens, 1976.
O'Neill, Mary	*Hailstones and Halibut Bones*. Doubleday, 1961.
Oppenheim, Joanne	*Mrs. Pelokis' Snake*. Dodd, 1980.
Orbach, Ruth	*Please Send a Panda*. Philomel, 1978.
Orlick, Terry	*The Cooperative Sports and Games Book: Challenge without Competition*. Pantheon, 1978.
Parish, Peggy	*Granny, the Baby, and the Big Gray Thing*. Macmillan, 1972.
Payne, Emmy	*Katy No-Pocket*. Houghton Mifflin, 1969.
Peet, Bill	*The Ant and the Elephant*. Houghton Mifflin, 1972. *Big Bad Bruce*. Houghton Mifflin, 1977. *Cowardly Clyde*. Houghton Mifflin, 1979. *Ella*. Houghton Mifflin, 1964. (p.b.) *Hubert's Hair-Raising Adventure*. Houghton Mifflin, 1959. (p.b.) *Jennifer and Josephine*. Houghton Mifflin, 1980. *Kermit the Hermit*. Houghton Mifflin, 1965. *The Wump World*. Houghton Mifflin, 1981.
Polhamus, Jean	*Dinosaur Funny Bones*. Prentice-Hall, 1974.
Quackenbush, Robert	*Henry's Awful Mistake*. Parents, 1981.
Radlauer, Ed	*Drag Racing*. Bowmar, 1967.
Radlauer, Ruth and Ed	*Hot Rod Mania*. Childrens, 1980. *On the Drag Strip*. Watts, 1971.

Ramage, Rosalyn	*A Book for All Seasons*. Broadman, 1977.
Reavin, Sam	*Hurray for Captain Jane*. Four Winds, 1971.
Reisberg, Ken	*Card Tricks*. Watts, 1980.
Riddell, James	*Animal Lore and Disorder: A Tops and Tales Menagerie*. Chatto Bodley Jonathan, 1980.
Rockwell, Anne	*The Awful Mess*. Four Winds, 1980.
	The Girl with a Donkey Tail. Dutton, 1979.
	Gollywhopper Egg. Macmillan, 1974.
	Gray Goose and Gander and Other Mother Goose Rhymes. Crowell, 1980.
	Tuhurahura and the Whale. Four Winds, 1971.
Ross, Wilda	*Can You Find the Animal?* Coward, 1974.
Ruben, Patricia	*Apples to Zippers: An Alphabet Book*. Doubleday, 1976.
	True or False? J. B. Lippincott, 1978.
	What Is New? What Is Missing? What Is Different? J. B. Lippincott, 1978.
Sattler, Helen	*No Place for a Goat*. Elsevier, 1982.
Schertle, Alice	*The Gorilla in the Hall*. Lothrop, 1977.
Schulz, Charles	*Happiness Is a Warm Puppy*. Determined Prods., 1979.
Scott, Beverly	*Santa's New Suit Funbook*. B. A. Scott, 1973. (p.b.)
Sendak, Maurice	*Hector Protector*. Harper & Row, 1965.
Shapp, Charles and Martha	*Let's Find Out about Fall*. Watts, 1963.
	Let's Find Out What's Big and What's Small. Watts, 1975.
Sharmat, Marjorie W.	*Burton and Dudley*. Holiday, 1975. (p.b.)
	Grumley the Grouch. Holiday, 1980.
	I'm Terrific. Holiday, 1977. (p.b.)
	Lucretia the Unbearable. Holiday, 1981.
	Mooch the Messy. Harper & Row, 1976.
	Nate the Great. Coward, 1972. (p.b.)
	Sophie and Gussie. Macmillan, 1973.
	Thornton the Worrier. Holiday, 1978.
	The 329th Friend. Four Winds, 1979.
	Walter the Wolf. Holiday, 1975.
Showers, Paul	*In the Night*. Crowell, 1961.

Silverstein, Shel

Giraffe and a Half. Harper & Row, 1964.

The Missing Piece. Harper & Row, 1976.

The Missing Piece Meets the Big O. Harper & Row, 1981.

Simon, Norma

I Know What I Like. Whitman, 1971.

Softly, Barbara

A Lemon Yellow Elephant Called Trunk. Harvey, n.d.

Spier, Peter

The Fox Went Out One Chilly Night. Doubleday, 1961. (p.b.)

People. Doubleday, 1980.

Tin Lizzie. Doubleday, 1978. (p.b.)

St. George, Judith

The Halloween Pumpkin Smasher. Putnam, 1978.

Stadler, John

Rodney and Lucinda's Amazing Race. Bradbury, 1981.

Steig, William

CDB. Windmill, 1968. (p.b.)

Storr, Catherine

Clever Polly and the Stupid Wolf. Faber & Faber, 1979.

Stubis, Patricia

Sandwichery: Recipes Riddles and Funny Facts about Food. Four Winds, 1975.

Thayer, Jane

Quiet on Account of a Dinosaur. Morrow, 1964.

Tison, Annette, and Talus Taylor

Barbapapa. Scholastic Book Services, 1979. (p.b.)

Tompert, Ann

Little Fox Goes to the End of the World. Crown, 1976. (p.b.)

Turk, Hanne

Hieronymus. Neugebauer, 1981.

Ungerer, Tomi

The Beast of Monsieur Racine. Farrar Straus & Giroux, 1971.

Crictor. Harper & Row, 1958. (p.b.)

Moon Man. Harper & Row, 1967.

No Kiss for Mother. Harper & Row, 1973.

Rufus. Harper & Row, 1961.

Snail, Where Are You? Harper & Row, 1962.

Zerelda's Ogre. Harper & Row, 1967.

Viorst, Judith

My Mama Says There Aren't Any Zombies, Ghosts, Vampires, Creatures, Demons, Monsters, Fiends, Goblins or Things. Atheneum, 1977. (p.b.)

Waber, Bernard

An Anteater Named Arthur. Houghton Mifflin, 1967 (p.b.)

Good-bye Funny Dumpy Lumpy. Houghton Mifflin, 1977.

I Was All Thumbs. Houghton Mifflin, 1975.

Ira Sleeps Over. Houghton Mifflin, 1972. (p.b.)

Lovable Lyle. Houghton Mifflin, 1969. (p.b.)

Rich Cat, Poor Cat. Scholastic Book Services, 1970.

Wegen, Ron   *Balloon Trip*. Houghton Mifflin, 1981.

Weston, Martha   *Peony's Rainbow*. Lothrop, 1981.

Willard, Nancy   *Simple Pictures Are Best*. Harcourt Brace Jovanovich, 1977.

Wilt, Joy   *The Nitty Gritty of Family Life*. Educational Products Division, 1979.

Wolcott, Patty   *Tunafish Sandwiches*. Addison-Wesley, 1975.

Young, Miriam   *If I Rode a Dinosaur*. Lothrop, 1974.

Zalben, Jane   *Norton's Nightime*. Philomel, 1979.
                            Will You Count the Stars without Me? Farrar Straus & Giroux, 1979.

Zemach, Margot   *To Hilda for Helping*. Farrar Straus & Giroux, 1977.

Index

The Aminal, 78
Andersen, Hans Christian, 13
Animal Research, 19, 99
Animals, 67, 73, 78, 80
Annie's Rainbow, 97
Anno, Mitsumasa, 15

Balian, Lorna, 78, 109
Barrett, Judi, 112
Bears, 21, 43
The Bed Just So, 48
Benarde, Anita, 35
Benjamin's 365 Birthdays, 112
The Biggest Sandwich Ever, 102
Birds, 123
Birthdays, 112
Boden, Alice, 95
A Book of Hugs, 52
Bookmarks, 24
Brooks, Ron, 97
Brown, Jeff, 24
The Bump in the Night, 37
Burningham, John, 119

Camouflage, 64
Card Games, 89
Cars, 76
Chaneles, Sol, 49
Charlip, Remy, 70
Christmas, 49, 55
*The Christmas Cookie Sprinkle
  Snitcher*, 55
Cities, 107
A Color of His Own, 64
Colors, 17, 64, 67, 97
Corduroy, 21
Crictor, 105

de Paola, Tomie, 82
de Regniers, Beatrice Schenk, 116
Dear Hildegarde, 99
Dinosaurs, 11

Easter, 109
*Eight Ate a Feast of Homonym
  Riddles*, 72
*"Elmer: The Story of a Patchwork
  Elephant,"* 67
Ernst, Kathryn, 30, 89

Fairy Tales, 13, 85, 116
Families, 57
The Field of Buttercups, 95
Flat Stanley, 24
Folktales, 37, 48, 73, 82
Freeman, Don, 21
Friendship, 28, 52, 70

Gelman, Rita Golden, 102
Grimm Brothers, 85
Guessing Games, 114, 125

Haas, Irene, 46
Halloween, 35
Hardendorff, Jeanne B., 48
*Harlequin and the Gift of Many
  Colors*, 70
Harold and the Purple Crayon, 17
Hawkesworth, Jenny, 107
Hoban, Tana, 114
Hoberman, Mary Ann, 32

Hogrogian, Nonny, 73
Homonyms, 72
A House Is a House for Me, 32
Humbug Rabbit, 109

I'm Terrific, 60
*The Ice Cream Cone Coot and
  Other Rare Birds*, 123
If the Dinosaurs Came Back, 11

Johnson, Crockett, 17

The King's Flower, 15
Kraus, Robert, 55

Letter Writing, 19, 99
Lionni, Leo, 64, 90
Listening, 62, 78, 119
The Little Red Balloon, 26
Lobel, Anita, 121
Lobel, Arnold, 123
The Lonely Skyscraper, 107
Look Again, 114

The Maggie B., 46
Mari, Iela, 26
Mayer, Mercer, 87
Monsters, 87
Most, Bernard, 11, 41, 80
Mr. Tamarin's Trees, 30
Mustaches, 92

My Daddy's Mustache, 92
My Very Own Octopus, 80

One Fine Day, 73
Orbach, Ruth, 19
Owl's New Cards, 89

Peet, Bill, 62
A Perfect Nose for Ralph, 43
Pezzettino, 90
Pinkwater, Daniel, 76
Please Send a Panda, 19
A Pocket for Corduroy, 21
The Princess and the Pea, 13
The Pumpkin Smasher, 35

Rainbows, 97
Rapunzel, 85

Recipes, 28
*Red Riding Hood: Retold in Verse
    for Boys and Girls*, 116
Rhyming Books, 32, 55, 123
Rockwell, Anne, 37
Ross, Dave, 52
Ruben, Patricia, 125

Salus, Naomi Panush, 92
Sandwiches, 102
Santa Makes a Change, 49
The Seamstress of Salzburg, 121
Seasons, 30
Self Esteem, 60
Shapes, 26, 46, 90
Sharmat, Marjorie Weiman, 28, 60
Snakes, 105
Spelling, 41, 72
St. Patrick's Day, 95
Strega Nona, 82

Tax, Meredith, 57
Terban, Marvin, 72
There's a Nightmare in My Closet,
    87
There's an Ant in Anthony, 41
The 329th Friend, 28
Tooth-Gnasher Superflash, 76
True or False?, 125

Ungerer, Tomi, 105

Waber, Bernard, 99
Wales, Katie, 67
The Whingdingdilly, 62
Would You Rather, 119

Zalben, Jane Breskin, 43

6 2 1 1 2 8 2 8 6

1 9 3 1 9 3 9 3 9 7

✗
9

1 7 4 8 0 6 8 7 4 8 7 2 5 3

1 7 4 8 0 6 8 7 4 8 7 2 5 3

answer